LOTUS® 1-2-3®
VERSION 2.2

Sarah E. Hutchinson
Stacey C. Sawyer
Glen J. Coulthard

THE IRWIN ADVANTAGE SERIES
FOR COMPUTER EDUCATION

♦

IRWIN

HOMEWOOD, IL 60430
BOSTON, MA 02116

Printed in the United States of America.

ISBN 0-256-13487-1

Lotus and Lotus 1-2-3 are registered trademarks of Lotus Development Corporation.

5 6 7 8 9 0 EB 0 9 8 7 6 5 4

CONTENTS

SESSION 1
LOTUS 1-2-3: FUNDAMENTALS 1

Why Is This Session Important? 3

Comparing Lotus Versions: 2.01 and 2.2 5

Parts of Lotus 1-2-3 and Add-Ins 6

Electronic Spreadsheet Development Procedures 6

Loading Lotus 1-2-3 8

Moving the Cursor 11

How the Keyboard Is Used in Lotus 1-2-3 12

Overview of Data Entry 13

    Entering Numbers and Text 15

    Entering Formulas 16

Editing a Cell 18

Using the UNDO Command (Version 2.2) 19

Using Menu Mode 20

Getting Help 21

Working with Ranges 23

Erasing a Range 23

Erasing the Spreadsheet Area 24

Exiting 25

Summary 26

Key Terms 27

Exercises 28

SESSION 2

LOTUS 1-2-3: WORKING WITH SPREADSHEETS 35

Why Is This Session Important? 37

Entering Text (Labels) 38

Entering Numbers (Values) 40

The @SUM Function 41

Formatting Numbers: Currency 43

Widening Columns 44

Changing the Current Directory 46

Saving the Spreadsheet 47

The SYSTEM Command 48

Recalculating the Spreadsheet: Changing a Few Numbers 49

Saving the Spreadsheet More Than Once 50

Retrieving the Spreadsheet 51

Printing the Spreadsheet 52

    As-Displayed Format 52

    Cell-Formulas Format 53

Print Options 55

    Using a Settings Sheet (Version 2.2) 57

    Headers and Footers 57

    Forcing a Page Break 59

Summary 60

Key Terms 62

Exercises 63

SESSION 3

LOTUS 1-2-3: ADDITIONAL SPREADSHEET PROCEDURES 69

Why Is This Session Important? 71

Copying 72

Copying Labels: Creating Underlines   73

Copying Formulas   75

Moving   78

Formatting Commands   80

Global Commands: Formatting Numbers and Widening Columns   82

Range Commands: Formatting Numbers and Realigning Labels   85

@AVG   86

@MIN   88

@MAX   88

@DATE   89

Calculating with Dates   93

@IF   94

Circular References: Avoid Them   96

Summary   99

Key Terms   100

Exercises   101

SESSION 4

LOTUS 1-2-3: MANAGING A SPREADSHEET   109

Why Is This Session Important?   111

Range Names   111

Titles   113

Setting Titles   114

Clearing Titles   116

Windows   117

Creating and Using a Window   117

Clearing the Window   119

Protection   119

Consolidating Spreadsheets   121

File-Linking (Version 2.2)   124

What Is a Macro?   126

Creating Macros   127

Creating a Save Macro   128

Creating Print Macros   130

Documenting Your Macros   132

Creating Macros Using Learn Mode   133

Creating a Save Macro   134

Creating Print Macros   136

Other Useful Macros   140

Summary   141

Key Terms   143

Exercises   144

SESSION 5

LOTUS 1-2-3: CREATING GRAPHS   149

Why Is This Session Important?   151

Forms of Business Graphics Presentation   151

Pie Charts   151

Line Charts   153

Bar Charts   154

XY Charts   155

Principles of Graphics Presentation   156

Simplicity   156

Unity   156

Emphasis   157

Balance   157

Saving Graphs: Important Steps to Follow   157

Using Lotus 1-2-3 to Create and Print Graphs 158

Creating a Pie Chart   161

Exploding and Shading   164

Creating a Simple Bar Chart   167

Creating a Stacked Bar Chart   169

Creating a Grouped Bar Chart   173

Creating a Line Chart   175

Creating a Table of Graph Names   176

Loading PrintGraph   177

Printing a Graph   179

Summary   180

Key Terms   181

Exercises   182

SESSION 6

LOTUS 1-2-3 ADD-INS: ALLWAYS AND THE MACRO LIBRARY MANAGER

189

Why Is This Session Important?   191

Using Add-In Software   193

Allways Fundamentals   193

   How Allways Uses the Keyboard   194

   Enhancing a Report   195

   Including a Graph in a Report   203

Macro Library Manager Fundamentals   205

   Creating and Using a Macro Library   206

Summary   208

Key Terms   210

Exercises   210

USING THIS GUIDE

This tutorial is one in a series of learning guides that lead you through the most popular microcomputer software programs available. Concepts, skills, and procedures are grouped into session topics and are presented in a logical and structured manner. Commands and procedures are introduced using hands-on examples, and you are encouraged to perform the steps along with the guide. Although you may turn directly to a later session, be aware that some sessions require, or at least assume, that you have completed the previous sessions. For maximum benefit, you should work through the short-answer and hands-on exercises appearing at the end of each session.

The exercises and examples in this guide use several standard conventions to indicate menu instructions, keystroke combinations, and command instructions.

MENU INSTRUCTIONS

When you need to execute a command from the Menu bar—the row of menu choices across the top of the screen—the tutorial's instruction line separates menu options with a comma. When you need to choose an option from a menu, we will display the name of the option with an underlined letter. (In Lotus, the underlined letter will always be the first letter of the command option.) For example, the command for retrieving a file is shown as:

CHOOSE: File, Retrieve

This instruction tells you to press the F key to choose the File option and then press the R key to choose the Retrieve option. Keys separated by commas are not pressed at the same time. (Note: We describe an additional method for choosing commands in the Using Menu Mode section in Session 1.)

KEYSTROKES AND KEYSTROKE COMBINATIONS

When you need to press two keys together, the tutorial's instruction line shows the keys joined with a plus sign (+). For example, to use the LEARN command in Lotus 1-2-3, hold down Alt and then press F5. The instruction for using the LEARN command is shown as:

PRESS: Alt+F5

COMMAND INSTRUCTIONS

This guide indicates with a special typeface data that you are required to type in yourself. For example:

    TYPE: George Washington

When you are required to enter unique information, such as the current date or your name, the instructions appear in italics. The following instruction directs you to type your name in place of the actual words: "your name."

    TYPE: *your name*

Instructions that use general directions rather than a specific option or command name appear italicized in the regular typeface.

    PRESS: *the cursor-movement keys to highlight the print range*

The Quick Reference sections may incorporate "syntax diagrams," which review standard command lines. Optional components of the command are placed in square brackets, similar to the following:

    Syntax: DIR [drive:][path][/p]/w]

This instrucion shows that the disk drive designation, path, /p, and/w choices are all optional. In other words, you can execute this command by entering DIR and then pressing the Enter key.

SESSION 1

LOTUS 1-2-3: FUNDAMENTALS

Be thankful for the electronic spreadsheet, one of the most commonly used tools in business! A few years ago, the spreadsheet was made out of paper and ink, was two feet across, and its 7,500 or so tiny spaces had to be filled in with tiny numbers by hand. Many a manager, accountant, or business planner consumed several weekends, cups of coffee, and resharpened pencils revising this paper instrument of torture. Today, the electronic version of the spreadsheet, such as Lotus, enables you to insert and change numbers with ease. This session shows you how to begin using this valuable tool.

PREVIEW

When you have completed this session, you will be able to:

Describe the different versions and parts of Lotus 1-2-3.
·
Describe the procedures required to create a reliable spreadsheet.
·
Load Lotus 1-2-3 and move the cursor.
·
Describe how the keyboard is used in Lotus 1-2-3.
·
Enter text, numbers, and formulas.
·
Explain the procedure involved with correcting errors.
·
Describe the UNDO command.
·
Use Lotus 1-2-3's menu system and help facility.
·
Work with spreadsheet ranges.
·
Erase spreadsheet cells.
·
Exit Lotus 1-2-3.

1

SESSION OUTLINE

Why Is This Session Important?
Comparing Lotus Versions: 2.01 and 2.2
Parts of Lotus 1-2-3 and Add-Ins
Electronic Spreadsheet Development Procedures
Loading Lotus 1-2-3
Moving the Cursor
How the Keyboard Is Used in Lotus 1-2-3
Overview of Data Entry
       Entering Numbers and Text
       Entering Formulas
Editing a Cell
Using the UNDO Command (Version 2.2)
Using Menu Mode
Getting Help
Working with Ranges
Erasing a Range
Erasing the Spreadsheet Area
Exiting
Summary
       Command Summary
Key Terms
Exercises
       Short Answer
       Hands-On

WHY IS THIS SESSION IMPORTANT?

This session leads you step-by-step through using one of the most popular spreadsheet applications available, Lotus 1-2-3. You'll concentrate initially on the fundamentals of spreadsheet design and construction and then explore the basic procedures, commands, and functions required to work effectively with the Lotus spreadsheet.

The electronic spreadsheet has been available for personal computers since the introduction of VisiCalc in 1978. Having sold over 400,000 copies, the VisiCalc program has been credited with driving the market for personal computers for several years after its introduction. With the arrival of Lotus 1-2-3 in 1983, the second generation of spreadsheet software was launched. Lotus expanded the perceived use of the electronic spreadsheet from a *visual calculator (VisiCalc)* to an all-around business tool, incorporating spreadsheet, graphing, and database capabilities into a single product.

For years, people used calculators and long scraps of paper to perform numerical calculations. However, the introduction of the electronic spreadsheet has almost rendered these tools obsolete for performing time-consuming, complicated calculations. Accountants, engineers, statisticians, and business people now use spreadsheet programs every day to analyze financial and statistical results.

An electronic spreadsheet is much more than a glorified calculator! Spreadsheets are often the primary tool used in financial decision-making, forecasting, and "what-if" analysis. Even though a spreadsheet can perform these multiple functions, the basics of creating a spreadsheet can be mastered quite quickly.

An electronic spreadsheet is similar to a manual worksheet, such as an accountant's pad. With a manual worksheet, items or accounts are usually listed in a row in the first column, and numbers are entered under column headings. An electronic spreadsheet is also comprised of rows and columns. The intersection of a row and column in an electronic spreadsheet is called a **cell**. When you construct a spreadsheet, you simply enter information into the individual cells.

One of the primary advantages of an electronic spreadsheet over a manual worksheet is the ability to perform **"what-if " analysis**. The term "what-if " refers to your ability to change information in the spreadsheet at any time and immediately see the effects of the change on other formulas or calculations. In other words, *"What if my sales were only 5,000 units? How would that affect my net income?"* or *"What if the interest rate was 8.5%? How would that affect my mortgage payment?"* Once the data has been entered into the spreadsheet, formulas can be created to sum a column of numbers, to calculate percentages, or to perform any number of calculations. These formulas often refer to locations, or **addresses**, of **cells** in a worksheet, as opposed to referring to the numbers themselves. When the data in a spreadsheet is changed, formulas are automatically recalculated.

Some additional advantages of electronic spreadsheets over manual worksheets include:

1. *Electronic spreadsheets can be larger than manual ones.*
    While a manual worksheet is limited to the size of the paper, an electronic spreadsheet is typically 256 columns by more than 8,000 rows. This expansive area allows you to keep related information together and to produce reports that are larger than a normal piece of paper. The computer screen can be thought of as a window on this large sheet of paper. Even though the spreadsheet has over 4,000,000 cells, moving the screen around the spreadsheet is fast and easy.

2. *Electronic spreadsheets can perform mathematical calculations.*
    A spreadsheet is used to calculate financial, statistical, and mathematical equations. **A formula** is a mathematical expression, such as 200+350, that is entered into a cell on the spreadsheet to display a result. This result may then be used in other formulas or printed out in a report. Any application that requires a calculator, a pen or a pencil, and an eraser can be handled by an electronic spreadsheet.

3. *Cells in electronic spreadsheets can contain formulas.*
    A spreadsheet cell may contain text, numbers, or formulas. A formula may consist solely of numbers or it may refer to other cells in the spreadsheet. Rather than containing the equation 200+350, a formula can specify references to the cells that contain these numbers. As a result, a new calculation is computed by simply entering new values in the cells where the old values appeared. As soon as the new numbers are entered, the spreadsheet recalculates the formula. Furthermore, you can create a spreadsheet before you accumulate all your information. Once the data is received and placed into the appropriate cells, the formulas will automatically perform the calculations.

4. *In electronic spreadsheets, calculations are immediate.*
    When you are working with a manual worksheet, changing a single number in a column can mean hours of extra work in recalculating totals, averages, and percentages by hand. Fortunately, an electronic spreadsheet allows you to create formulas using cell addresses rather than the actual numbers. Therefore, changing a number in a cell produces a ripple effect of recalculations for all formulas depending on that one cell.

5. *Electronic spreadsheets can be stored and retrieved.*
    An electronic spreadsheet can be permanently saved on diskettes, hard disks, tape drives, and several other types of media for safe storage. Rather than having to search through endless filing cabinets for manual worksheets created months before, you can use your computer's electronic filing system to search for and retrieve files instantaneously. An electronic spreadsheet can be

retrieved, edited, updated, printed, and then saved under a new name quickly and easily.

COMPARING LOTUS VERSIONS: 2.01 AND 2.2

The sessions in this guide can be used with versions 2.01 and 2.2 of Lotus 1-2-3. The command keystrokes are the same no matter which version you are using; however, version 2.2 includes some new capabilities:

- With version 2.2, cells in one spreadsheet file can be linked with cells in another spreadsheet file. A change in one spreadsheet is automatically reflected in the other spreadsheet. File-linking is described in Session 4.

- A few special enhancements make version 2.2 easier to use than version 2.01. For example, with version 2.2 you can simultaneously adjust the width of several columns.

- The quality of your printed reports and graphs is greatly improved with version 2.2 because of an add-in program called Allways, which is stored in RAM at the same time as Lotus 1-2-3. *Allways* provides a number of commands for "dressing up" your reports.

- Version 2.2 provides users with the capability to "undo" a change or a command that was issued by mistake. (The UNDO command is described in more detail later in this session.)

- Version 2.2 makes it much easier for users to create macros. (Macros are used to automate procedures and thus reduce the number of keystrokes needed to execute those procedures.) The steps for creating macros are described in Session 4.

The Lotus 1-2-3 screen looks almost the same in both versions. The screen images in this guide were generated using version 2.2.

Before proceeding, make sure the following are true:

1. You have access to version 2.01 or 2.2 of Lotus 1-2-3.

2. Your Advantage Diskette is inserted in the drive. You will save your work onto the diskette and retrieve the files that have been created for you. (Note: The Advantage Diskette can be made by copying all the files off the instructor's Master Advantage Diskette onto a formatted diskette.)

PARTS OF LOTUS 1-2-3 AND ADD-INS

Lotus 1-2-3 provides users with four categories of capabilities:

1. *Spreadsheet.* Lotus's spreadsheet capabilities enable you to enter text and numbers and to then perform calculations—using formulas—on the data you have typed in. When a number is changed in the spreadsheet, the formulas automatically calculate the new results. Lotus's spreadsheet capabilities are described in Sessions 1–4.

2. *Database.* With Lotus's database capabilities, you can sort data into order and retrieve information from a base of data. Compared with other types of database programs, manipulating data with an electronic spreadsheet program is faster because the entire database is stored in RAM during processing. With other programs, portions of the database are stored on disk, which can slow processing down.

3. *Graphics.* Lotus's graphics capabilities enable you to present data in the form of business charts, including pie charts, bar charts, line charts, and XY charts. People often understand data more readily when it is presented in graphic form. Lotus's graphics capabilities are described in Session 5.

4. *Add-ins.* Allways enables you to output spreadsheets with presentation-quality characteristics—that is, more professional looking and easier to read than ordinary spreadsheets. In addition, Allways enables you to merge text and graphics on a single page. The Macro Library Manager add-in enables you to store the macros you create in a file that can be accessed from all your spreadsheets, which can ultimately save you time. Lotus's add-ins are described in more detail in Session 6.

ELECTRONIC SPREADSHEET DEVELOPMENT PROCEDURES

Specific guidelines have evolved for developing electronic spreadsheets on the basis of the collective experience of the many people who have built them. *If you take shortcuts instead of following these procedures, you will develop spreadsheets that aren't reliable.* Recent studies done by several major universities found that 90% of all spreadsheets developed by nonprogramming professionals contained at least one error. And business decisions are being made on the basis of spreadsheets like these!

The steps for consistently developing a reliable spreadsheet are as follows:

1. *Establish your objectives.*
   Ask yourself why you are creating a spreadsheet. Is it to save time from lengthy calculations or to provide a regular template for a monthly report? By expressly stating your objectives, you gain a better understanding of the requirements of the spreadsheet. Remember, not everything needs to be computerized!

2. *Define the output requirements.*
   The layout or structure of a spreadsheet is largely determined by the types of reports required. Try to mock up the reports on paper before creating the spreadsheet. This helps determine the best layout for the spreadsheet.

3. *Construct the spreadsheet.*
   Having completed your needs assessment in steps 1 and 2, begin constructing the spreadsheet. The majority of spreadsheet users enter the "known" information first, whether text or numbers, and then proceed with creating formulas. This process allows you to see the results of a formula calculation immediately upon its entry.

4. *Test the spreadsheet.*
   Testing involves performing manual calculations on separate parts of the spreadsheet and then comparing those values with the spreadsheet's results. Do not take it for granted that the spreadsheet calculations are correct. As mentioned previously, a simple mistake in typing can cause a ripple effect of incorrect results across an entire spreadsheet.

5. *Use the spreadsheet.*
   A spreadsheet is often designed with unclear objectives, or the objectives may change after the spreadsheet is constructed. Therefore, the use and reuse of a spreadsheet is important in providing feedback for enhancements and modifications. A spreadsheet is a dynamic tool—it must be updated and maintained to remain relevant. However, before modifying a spreadsheet, make sure that you have made backup copies of the original.

6. *Document the spreadsheet.*
   A spreadsheet can become quite complex. Proper documentation is essential, especially when the spreadsheet is used by several different people. Documentation consists of on-screen and paper instructions specifying where and how information is to be entered and outlining the formulas used to perform calculations.

LOADING LOTUS 1-2-3

This session assumes that you are working on a computer with DOS and Lotus loaded on the hard disk drive. In most cases, the hard disk of a personal computer is drive C:. Lotus 1-2-3 is probably loaded in a subdirectory (named \LOTUS or \123) on the hard disk, which is often included in the path statement of the AUTOEXEC batch file.

1. First, turn the computer on. Turn on the power switches to the computer and monitor. The C:\> prompt or a menu appears announcing that your computer has successfully loaded DOS.

2. To load Lotus 1-2-3, use one of the following methods:
    a. If a menu is displaying on the screen that contains an option for Lotus, choose the Lotus option. The screen should look like Figure 1.1.
    b. If the C:\> prompt is displaying on the screen:
        TYPE: lotus
        PRESS: (Enter)
        Your screen should look like Figure 1.1.

Figure 1.1

The Lotus Access System

```
┌─────────────────────────────────────────────────────────────────┐
│ 1-2-3  PrintGraph  Translate  Install  Exit                       │
│ Use 1-2-3                                                          │
├───────────────────────────────────────────────────────────────── │
│                                                                   │
│  ┌─────────────────────────────────────────────────────────────┐ │
│                     1-2-3 Access System                           │
│                   Copyright  1986, 1989                           │
│                Lotus Development Corporation                      │
│                     All Rights Reserved                           │
│                        Release 2.2                                │
│                                                                   │
│   The Access system lets you choose 1-2-3, PrintGraph, the Translate utility, │
│   and the Install program, from the menu at the top of this screen.  If │
│   you're using a two-diskette system, the Access system may prompt you to │
│   change disks.  Follow the instructions below to start a program. │
│                                                                   │
│   o  Use → or ← to move the menu pointer (the highlighted rectangle │
│      at the top of the screen) to the program you want to use.    │
│                                                                   │
│   o  Press ENTER to start the program.                            │
│                                                                   │
│   You can also start a program by typing the first character of its name. │
│                                                                   │
│   Press HELP (F1) for more information.                           │
│  └─────────────────────────────────────────────────────────────┘ │
└───────────────────────────────────────────────────────────────── ┘
```

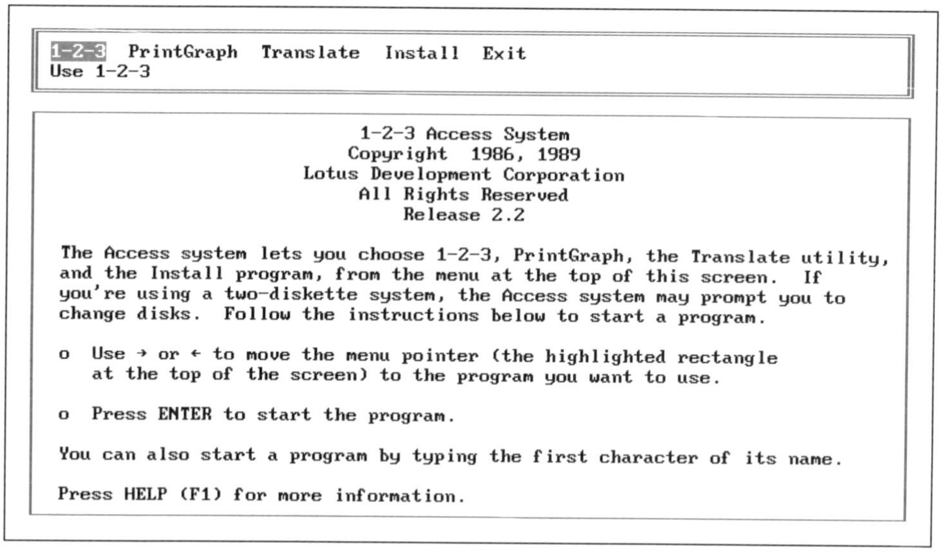

You are looking at the Lotus Access System. The cursor is currently highlighting the 1-2-3 option, and a description of this option is on the second line.

The PrintGraph option is used for printing the graphs you create (you will use this option in Session 5).

The Translate option enables you to transfer data from another software application into Lotus 1-2-3 so that it can be manipulated using Lotus 1-2-3's commands.

When you first purchase Lotus 1-2-3, you must use the Install option to tell the program about the characteristics of your hardware. (For example, will you use Lotus 1-2-3 on a microcomputer configured with a color monitor? What kind of printer will you use?) By choosing the Exit option, you exit the Lotus Access System.

Two methods can be used to choose an option from a Lotus menu. You can either highlight the option (using the cursor-movement keys) and then press Enter, *or press the first character of the option.*

3. The cursor should still be highlighting the 1-2-3 option. To choose this option:
   PRESS: Enter
   The screen should look like Figure 1.2.

Figure 1.2

The Lotus 1-2-3 spreadsheet

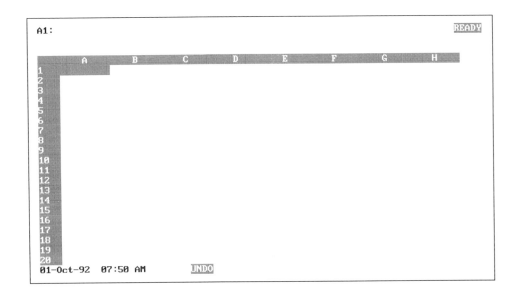

Quick Reference

Loading Lotus 1-2-3

After the system prompt:
TYPE: lotus
PRESS: Enter

To choose the 1-2-3 option:
PRESS: Enter

What do you see? Figure 1.3 explains what you see on the Lotus 1-2-3 screen. Across the top of your screen you should see the letters A–H, and down the left side of the screen you should see the numbers 1–20. These are the column and row references you will use to identify a cell (the intersection between a column and row). For example, F6 means column F and row 6. In the upper-right corner of the screen is a mode indicator that says READY. When Lotus is in **Ready mode,** it is ready for you to move the cursor and then type data into the cells in the spreadsheet. Table 1.1 describes the different modes that Lotus operates in.

Figure 1.3

The Lotus 1-2-3
screen

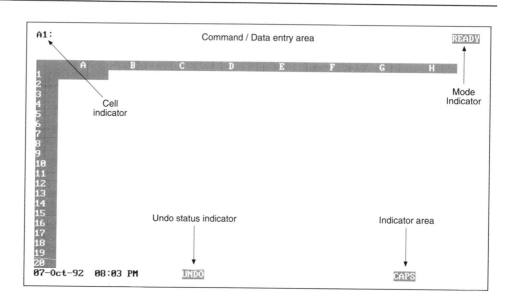

Table 1.1	Edit	You are changing the contents of a cell after either making a mistake in a formula or using F2.
Lotus 1-2-3 Modes of Operation (Partial List)	Files	You are displaying a list of files on the screen.
	Help	You have pressed F1.
	Mem	Lotus warns you with this indicator when the amount of available main memory (RAM) in your computer drops below 4096 bytes.

Table 1.1	Ovr	You have pressed [Insert], which toggles Insert mode off. As a result, what you type will overwrite existing data rather than be inserted at the current cursor location.
Lotus 1-2-3 Modes of Operation (concluded)	Ready	You can move the cursor around the spreadsheet. Lotus 1-2-3 is "ready" for you to type something into a cell or issue a command.
	Label	You are in the process of typing text into a cell.
	Menu	You have pressed the slash (/) key to display the Lotus 1-2-3 menu.
	Point	You are in the process of using a Lotus 1-2-3 command and are highlighting a range of cells.
	Undo	The Undo feature of Lotus 1-2-3 is activated.
	Value	You are in the process of typing a number or formula into a cell.

MOVING THE CURSOR

The cursor is now positioned in cell A1. To create spreadsheets, you must first know how to move the cursor using the cursor-movement keys. Table 1.2 lists a few different ways of moving the cursor.

Perform the following steps:

1. To move the cursor to cell G1, press ⟶ six times.

2. To move the cursor to cell J1, press ⟶ three more times. You can always tell what cell the cursor is in by looking at the cell identifier in the upper-left corner of the screen.

What has happened to columns A and B? They have scrolled off the screen to the left. Your screen is a "window" through which you are viewing a portion of a very large spreadsheet.

3. To move the cursor to cell J21, press ⟶ 20 times. Note that row 1 has now scrolled off the top of the screen.

Table 1.2	[Home]	Moves the cursor to cell A1 from anywhere in the spreadsheet.
Moving the Cursor	[End]	When used before any of the arrow keys, it will move you to the last cell in a range of empty or filled cells.
	[←] [→]	Used to move the cursor either left or right one column.
	[↑] [↓]	Used to move the cursor either up or down one row.
	[PgUp]	Used to move the cursor up an entire screen.
	[PgDn]	Used to move the cursor down an entire screen.
	[Tab]	Moves the cursor a screen to the right.
	[Shift]+[Tab]	Moves the cursor a screen to the left.
	[F5]	Enables you to go to a cell directly. After pressing [F5], type the cell reference you want to go to and then press [Enter].

4. Fortunately, there is an easier way to move the cursor up and down 20 rows at a time—using [PgUp] and [PgDn].
    PRESS: [PgDn] *twice*
    The cursor should now be in cell J61.
    PRESS: [PgUp]
    The cursor should now be in cell J41.

5. [Home] gets you back to cell A1.
    PRESS: [Home]
    The cursor should again be in cell A1.

As you can see, moving the cursor around the spreadsheet is simple. To create a spreadsheet, you must move the cursor to the appropriate cell before typing anything.

HOW THE KEYBOARD IS USED IN LOTUS 1-2-3

Listed below is a description of how some of the keys on the keyboard are used in Lotus 1-2-3. Because you are new to Lotus 1-2-3, you might not at first understand how some of these keys work. However, after completing this guide, you will understand how to use most of the keys described here.

- The **slash key** (/) is used to display the Lotus 1-2-3 menu on the top of the screen.

- If you accidentally choose a command on a menu, you can move out of that menu option by pressing the **Escape key** (Esc).

- When you are typing letters or numbers, use BackSpace to delete the character or space to the left.

- When you are typing letters or numbers, use Delete to delete the character or space the cursor is positioned on.

- Use Enter to put data into a cell and to choose a command after a command option has been highlighted on the Lotus 1-2-3 menu.

- Use the **period key** (.) to specify a range of cells—that is, a group of cells that forms a rectangle (ranges are described shortly).

- The **Alternate key** (Alt) is also used in conjunction with the function keys to execute commands.

- The function keys are described in Table 1.3.

OVERVIEW OF DATA ENTRY

In this section we describe some of the fundamentals of entering text, numbers, formulas, and functions in the cells of a spreadsheet. No matter what you are typing into a cell, you must remember to first move the cursor to the appropriate cell, type what you want to put in the cell, and then press Enter or one of the cursor-movement keys (↑, ↓, ←, →, PgUp, PgDn).

Lotus looks at the first character you type to see whether it's a label (text) or a value. If the first character you type is an alphabetic character, Lotus goes into **Label mode**. Lotus goes into **Value mode** if the first character you type is either a number or one of the following characters:

+   −   (@   .   # $

You can tell what mode Lotus is in by looking in the upper-right corner of the spreadsheet.

Table 1.3 Description of the Function Keys	F1 HELP	Press this key to call up help information on the screen.
	F2 Edit	Press this key to edit the cell on which the cursor is positioned.
	F3 NAME	Press this key to display a list of range names on the screen.
	F4 ABS	Use this key to prepare a formula before it is copied by defining a cell as an absolute reference.
	F5 GOTO	Use this key to move the cursor directly to any cell in the spreadsheet.
	F6 WINDOW	Use this key to switch between windows.
	F7 QUERY	Use this key to simplify the process of using the DATA QUERY EXTRACT or the DATA QUERY FIND command. These are database commands.
	F8 TABLE	This key simplifies the process of using the DATA TABLE command. This is a database command.
	F9 CALC	When the recalculation method has been changed from automatic to manual, press this key to recalculate all the formulas in the spreadsheet.
	F10 GRAPH	Press this key to display the last graph you created on the screen.
	Alt+F2 STEP	This command allows you to execute a macro one command at a time.
	Alt+F3 RUN	Use this command to display a list of macro names to choose from.
	Alt+F4 UNDO	Use this command to cancel any changes that were made to a spreadsheet since the spreadsheet was last in Ready mode.
	Alt+F5 LEARN	Use this command to record (in a range of cells) as text the keys you press and the commands you execute—this text is then used as a macro.
	Alt+F10 ADD-IN	This command enables you to use an add-in program such as Allways. (Allways is described in Session 6, and the Macro Library Manager is described in Session 6.)

ENTERING NUMBERS AND TEXT

Keying in numbers and text is simple.

Entering numbers:

1. The cursor should be positioned in cell A1.
    TYPE: 10
    PRESS: [Enter]
    The number 10 should be displaying in cell A1. Note that the number appears on the right side of the cell. Lotus always positions numbers (values) on the right side of a cell and text (labels) on the left side of a cell. If you look in the upper-left corner of the screen, you can see that cell A1 contains the number 10.

2. Using the cursor-movement keys, position the cursor in cell A2.

3. TYPE: 20
    PRESS: [Enter]

4. Position the cursor in cell A3.

5. TYPE: 30
    PRESS: [↓]
    The number 30 was entered into cell A3 and the cursor moved down one cell. As mentioned earlier, *the cursor-movement keys can be used to enter data and information into a cell.*

6. Now we'll show you how easy it is to change the contents of a cell. Position the cursor in cell A1.

7. TYPE: 25
    PRESS: [Enter]
    The number 25 replaced the number 10. Positioning the cursor on a cell and typing new contents is one method of editing the contents of a cell.

Entering text:

1. Position the cursor in cell B1.

2. TYPE: xyz
    PRESS: [Enter]
    If you look at the upper-left corner of the screen, you can see that xyz is stored in the cell. Note that Lotus automatically supplied an apostrophe before the letters. *Lotus uses the apostrophe to represent left-alignment in the cell. The quotation mark (") stands for right-alignment, and the caret (^) stands for center-alignment.*

3. Position the cursor in cell B2.

4. TYPE: "xyz
   PRESS: [Enter]
   The characters xyz should be displaying on the right side of the cell.

5. Position the cursor in cell B3.

6. TYPE: ^xyz
   PRESS: [Enter]
   The characters xyz should be displaying in the center of the cell.

....

Quick Reference   1. Use the cursor-movement keys to position the cursor in the appropriate
                               cell.
Entering Numbers   2. TYPE: *the number(s) or text*
and Text   3. PRESS: [Enter]
                               or
                               PRESS: *a cursor-movement key*

....

The text or numbers you type in a cell are often wider than the column. Lotus's default column width is nine characters. (The term *default* refers to the assumptions made by Lotus until the user tells it otherwise.) Because users often have to change column width, spreadsheet programs provide the user with a command that performs this task. For instance, look at Figure 1.4; cell A3 contains the text "INCOME AND EXPENSE BUDGET SPREADSHEET" (you can tell which cell the cursor is in by looking at the upper-left corner of the screen), and cell B3 contains the text 1992–1993. Because the columns haven't been widened—that is, the default column width values are in effect—you can't see all of the text in cell A3. Cell A1 contains "ABRAHAMSON AND BOWMAN TEXTILE COMPANY"; even though cell B1 appears to contain "AND BOWMAN," it actually contains nothing. The text in cell A1 is borrowing space from the right. We can see all of the text in cell A1 because cell B1 is empty. We'll change column widths in Session 2.

ENTERING FORMULAS

A formula is a mathematical expression that enables you to perform calculations on values in a spreadsheet. Table 1.4 shows the logical and arithmetic operators that can be used in Lotus 1-2-3 formulas. These operators are similar to those found in most electronic spreadsheet programs.

Figure 1.4

Hidden cell
contents

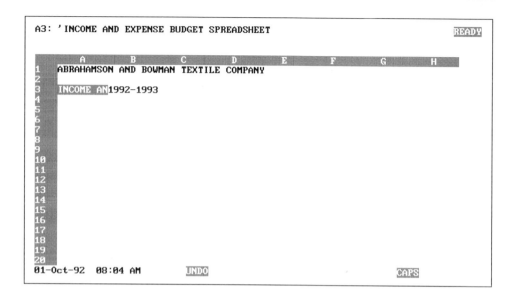

```
A3: 'INCOME AND EXPENSE BUDGET SPREADSHEET                          READY

            A          B         C        D        E      F       G       H
 1   ABRAHAMSON AND BOWMAN TEXTILE COMPANY
 2
 3   INCOME AN 1992-1993
 4
 5
 6
 7
 8
 9
10
11
12
13
14
15
16
17
18
19
20
01-Oct-92   08:04 AM              UNDO                              CAPS
```

Table 1.4

Formula
operators

Logical Operators	
=	Equal
<	Less than
<=	Less than or equal to
>	Greater than
>=	Greater than or equal to
<>	Not equal
#NOT#	Not
#AND#	And
#OR#	Or

Arithmetic Operators		Example
+	Addition	+A1+A2
-	Subtraction	+A1-A2
*	Multiplication	+A1*A2
/	Division	+A1/A2

Perform the following steps to put a formula in cell A4 that will add the amounts in the three cells above it:

1. Position the cursor in cell A4.

2. TYPE: +A1+A2+A3
    Watch the left top corner of the screen. If you make a mistake typing in the
    formula, use (BackSpace) to delete what you typed; then start over.
    PRESS: (Enter)

The number displayed in cell A4 should be the total of cells A1, A2, and A3.

CAUTION: If the formula you typed in cell A4 didn't include a beginning plus
sign (+), Lotus assumed you were typing a label, because the first character is an
alphabetic character. The plus sign forces Lotus into Value mode, which is
necessary to enter formulas.

Editing a Cell

What if you type text, a number, or a formula into a cell and then decide it needs
to be changed? Two methods can be used to edit the contents of a cell in a
spreadsheet.

Method One: Position the cursor on the cell that needs to be changed. Retype the
contents. Press (Enter). Once you press (Enter), what you typed will replace what
was formerly in the cell. This method is best if you need to completely replace the
contents of a cell.

Method Two: Position the cursor on the cell that needs to be changed. Press (F2)
(Edit). The contents of the cell the cursor is positioned on will appear above the
spreadsheet area so that you can edit it. Make your changes, and then press
(Enter). This method is best if you need to make only a few changes to the
contents of a cell, or if you're editing a cell that contains many characters.

To practice using (F2), perform the following steps:

1. Position the cursor in cell B1.

2. In this step you will edit the contents of cell B1 so that instead of displaying
    'xyz in the cell, cell B1 will display 'xyz company.
    PRESS: (F2)
    A copy of the contents of cell B1 ('xyz) should be displaying on the top of the
    screen.
    PRESS: Space Bar
    TYPE: company
    PRESS: (Enter)
    The text 'xyz company should now be displaying in the cell.

Quick Reference	Method 1:
	1. Position the cursor on the cell that needs to be changed.
Editing a Cell	2. TYPE: *what you want in the cell*
	PRESS: (Enter)

Method 2:
1. Position the cursor on the cell that needs to be changed.
2. PRESS: (F2)
3. A copy of the contents of the cell will appear on the data entry line. Make any changes, and then press (Enter).

USING THE UNDO COMMAND (VERSION 2.2)

(Skip to the Using Menu Mode section if you are using version 2.01 or if UNDO isn't displaying on the bottom of your screen.) The **UNDO command** enables you to cancel any changes you have made to a spreadsheet since you were last in Ready mode. This command is useful if, for example, you accidentally enter some text into a cell that contained a formula. You can bring the formula back into the cell using the UNDO command. When you use this command, your spreadsheet must be in Ready mode. Then hold (Alt) down and press (F4).

To practice, perform the following steps:

1. Position the cursor in cell A4, which currently contains a formula.

2. TYPE: hello
   PRESS: (Enter)

3. Note that the word "hello" now appears in cell A4. To bring the formula back:
   PRESS: (Alt)+(F4)
   (Note: As mentioned previously, when a plus sign appears between two keys, hold the first key down and then press the second key. In this instance, hold (Alt) down and then press (F4). The formula again appears in the cell. Use the UNDO command again and the word "hello" will appear in the cell. Use the UNDO command once more so that the formula is again in the cell.

Quick Reference	To see what your spreadsheet looked like when it was last in Ready mode:
UNDO (Alt)+(F4)	PRESS: (Alt)+(F4)
	To return to your current spreadsheet version:
	PRESS: (Alt)+(F4)

USING MENU MODE

Lotus 1-2-3's commands are organized hierarchically, which means that subselections exist in a menu of choices under the main command headings. To enter **Menu mode,** you must press the slash (/) key. To practice using Lotus's menus, perform the following steps:

1. To enter Menu mode:
    TYPE: /
    Note that the mode indicator changed to MENU.

2. The cursor is highlighting the Worksheet option. The second line, below "Worksheet" lists the Worksheet group of commands.
    PRESS: →

3. The cursor is now highlighting the Range option, and a list of the Range group of commands is on the line below. *As you highlight a menu option, a description of that option appears on the line below. To choose an option, press* (Enter) *when an option is highlighted. By proceeding in this fashion, you go deeper and deeper into Lotus's hierarchical command structure.*

4. To choose the Worksheet group of commands, highlight WORKSHEET and press (Enter). The cursor should now be highlighting the Global option. To choose this option, press (Enter). The cursor should be highlighting the Format option. To choose this option, press (Enter). Now you are in the "Fixed" option. Note that you are moving deeper into the command hierarchy. If for some reason you don't want to complete a command, press (Esc) to move back up the command structure until the spreadsheet is again in Ready mode.
    PRESS: (Esc) *until the mode indicator says READY*

5. You can also choose command options by pressing the first character of the option. To illustrate:
    TYPE: /
    To choose the File option:
    TYPE: F
    To choose the Directory option:
    TYPE: D
    To return to Ready mode:
    PRESS: (Esc) *until the mode indicator says READY*

In the sessions in this guide, you can choose commands using either method. For example, to indicate that you should use the WORKSHEET ERASE command, you will see:

CHOOSE: Worksheet, Erase

You can use the slash key (/) plus the cursor-movement keys and (Enter), *or use the slash key followed by W and then E.*

Quick Reference

Using Menu Mode

1. PRESS: /
2. To choose an option, either use the cursor-movement keys to highlight the option and then press (Enter), or type the first character of the option and then press (Enter).
3. To back out of an option or to get back to Ready mode: PRESS: (Esc)

GETTING HELP

Since Lotus 1-2-3 provides over 115 commands for you to use, you probably won't be able to remember how to use all of them. If you find yourself in the middle of a command but aren't sure how to use it, use the **Help facility,** which provides information about each of Lotus's commands. The Help facility is accessed by pressing the Help key ((F1)).

Perform the following steps to use the Help facility:

1. The spreadsheet should be in Ready mode (check the mode indicator in the upper-right corner).

2. PRESS: (F1)
   If you press (F1) while the spreadsheet is in Ready mode, the screen pictured in Figure 1.5 will display. To retrieve information about a particular command, you can highlight the command using the cursor-movement keys; then press (Enter). To return to Ready mode, press (Esc).

3. PRESS: (Esc) *until the spreadsheet is again in Ready mode*

4. To illustrate what happens when you press (F1) while in Menu mode:
   TYPE: /
   PRESS: (F1)
   Because the cursor is highlighting the Worksheet group of commands, pressing (F1) provides information about the Worksheet group of commands (Figure 1.6).

Figure 1.5

This Lotus 1-2-3 help screen was accessed from Ready mode by pressing [F1].

```
A4:  +A1+A2+A3                                                         HELP


─────────────────────────────────────────────────────────────────────────

1-2-3 Help Index

About 1-2-3 Help          Linking Files              1-2-3 Main Menu
Cell Formats              Macro Basics               /Add-In
Cell/Range References     Macro Command Index        /Copy
Column Widths             Macro Key Names            /Data
Control Panel             Mode Indicators            /File
Entering Data             Operators                  /Graph
Error Message Index       Range Basics               /Move
Formulas                  Recalculation              /Print
@Function Index           Specifying Ranges          /Quit
Function Keys             Status Indicators          /Range
Keyboard Index            Task Index                 /System
Learn Feature             Undo Feature               /Worksheet

─────────────────────────────────────────────────────────────────────────

To select a topic, press a pointer-movement key to highlight the topic and then
press ENTER.  To return to a previous Help screen, press BACKSPACE.  To leave
Help and return to the worksheet, press ESC.

01-Oct-92   08:56 AM
```

Figure 1.6

If you press [F1] while highlighting a command, Lotus will display a help screen that relates to the command.

```
A4:  +A1+A2+A3                                                         HELP
Worksheet  Range  Copy  Move  File  Print  Graph  Data  System  Add-In  Quit
Global  Insert  Delete  Column  Erase  Titles  Window  Status  Page  Learn

1-2-3 Commands

Worksheet Commands         Graph Commands
Range Commands             Data Commands
/Copy                      /System
/Move                      Add-In Commands
File Commands              /Quit
Print Commands

To use 1-2-3 commands, type / (slash) or < (less-than symbol) to display the
main menu at the top of the screen.

To select a command from the menu, highlight the command and press ENTER or
type the first character of the command.  When you highlight a command, 1-2-3
displays an explanation or submenu in the third line of the control panel.

To back out of a menu one level at a time, press ESC.
To leave a menu and return to READY mode, press CTRL-BREAK.

Using Command Menus                                           Help Index
01-Oct-92   09:00 AM
```

5. To exit the help facility:
    PRESS: [Esc] *until the spreadsheet is again in Ready mode*

....

Quick Reference

Using Help [F1]

1. In Ready mode, press [F1] to display a list of commands. Press [Enter] to display additional information about a highlighted command.

2. In Menu mode, press [F1] to display information about the highlighted command.

....

WORKING WITH RANGES

Many of Lotus's commands involve specifying what cell or cells you want to perform a command on. If the cells form a rectangle, it is referred to as a **range**. A single cell can also be used as a range. Figure 1.7 highlights a number of different spreadsheet ranges. The beginning and end of a range is separated by two dots, or periods (..). In the next section you learn how to erase a range of cells.

Figure 1.7

Spreadsheet ranges

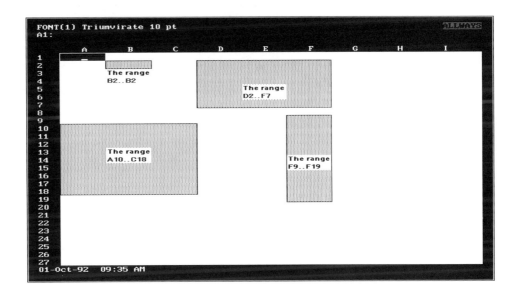

ERASING A RANGE

A commonly performed spreadsheet procedure is to erase an individual cell or a range of cells. For example, you might type something into a cell and later decide you want the cell to appear blank. The **RANGE ERASE** command enables you to erase the contents of one or more cells.

In the following steps you will use the RANGE ERASE command to erase the range B1..B2. Before using the RANGE ERASE command, position the cursor at the beginning of the range to be erased.

1. Position the cursor on cell B1.

2. TYPE: /
    CHOOSE: Range, Erase

3. To highlight and then erase the range B1..B2:
    PRESS: ⬇
    B1..B2 should be displaying in the range to erase in the top-left corner of the
    screen (Figure 1.8).
    PRESS: Enter
    The contents of range B1..B2 should now be gone.

Figure 1.8

Erasing a range

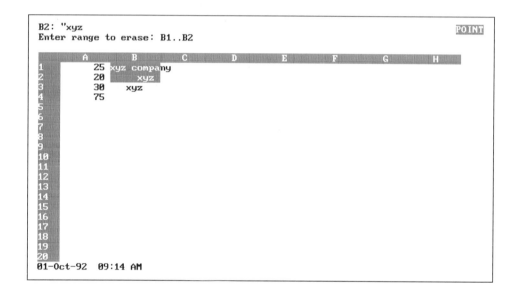

```
B2: "xyz                                                                    POINT
Enter range to erase: B1..B2
        A         B         C         D         E         F         G         H
1          25 xyz company
2          20      xyz
3          30    xyz
4          75
5
6
7
8
9
10
11
12
13
14
15
16
17
18
19
20
01-Oct-92   09:14 AM
```

In subsequent sessions, use the RANGE ERASE command if you need to erase
the contents of one or more cells in a spreadsheet.

Quick Reference

Erasing a Range

1. Position the cursor at the beginning of the range to be erased.
2. To enter Menu mode:
    TYPE: /
3. CHOOSE: Range, Erase
4. Use the cursor-movement keys to highlight the range of cells to be erased
    and then press Enter.

ERASING THE SPREADSHEET AREA

To erase the entire spreadsheet contents from the screen so you can begin work on
another spreadsheet, use the **WORKSHEET ERASE** command. You would

typically save your work before erasing the spreadsheet area; however, in this session, we treat the spreadsheet as a practice area.

Perform the following steps to erase the spreadsheet area:

1. To enter Menu mode:
    TYPE: /

2. CHOOSE: Worksheet, Erase, Yes
    Your screen should look like it did when you first loaded Lotus.

....

Quick Reference   1.   To enter Menu mode:
Erasing the   TYPE: /
Spreadsheet Area   2.   CHOOSE: Worksheet, Erase, Yes

....

CAUTION: Make sure you use the RANGE ERASE command to erase one or more cells rather than the WORKSHEET ERASE command. The WORKSHEET ERASE command will erase the contents of every cell in the spreadsheet.

EXITING

Before you exit Lotus 1-2-3, you should save your work. However, since the data from your spreadsheet was erased in the last section, you don't need to save now. (In Session 2, you will learn how to save a spreadsheet.)

Perform the following steps to exit Lotus 1-2-3:

1. To enter Menu mode:
    TYPE: /

2. CHOOSE: Quit, Yes
    (If your spreadsheet hadn't been empty, Lotus would have displayed a prompt asking if you wanted to exit 1-2-3 without saving.)

3. The Lotus Access System menu should appear at the top of the screen. To exit this menu:
    CHOOSE: Exit
    The DOS prompt now displays.

....

Quick Reference	1.	TYPE: /
	2.	CHOOSE: <u>Q</u>uit, <u>Y</u>es
Exiting Lotus 1-2-3	3.	If your spreadsheet isn't empty, Lotus will now ask if you want to save your changes. Choose Yes or No.
	4.	CHOOSE: <u>E</u>xit

....

In the next session you will practice creating, editing, saving, and printing a spreadsheet.

SUMMARY

Now that you've learned the basics of creating a spreadsheet, you are prepared to proceed with Session 2, which leads you through creating a spreadsheet that keeps track of quarterly expenses. As you proceed with the sessions in this guide, don't forget to use the Help key ([F1]) if you need more information about a particular menu option.

COMMAND SUMMARY

The following table provides a list of the commands and procedures covered in this session.

Table 1.5	Load Lotus 1-2-3	Type LOTUS after the system prompt and press [Enter]. Press [Enter] to choose the 1-2-3 option.
Command Summary	Move the cursor	Use the cursor-movement keys, [PgUp], [PgDn], [Home], [End], [Tab], and [F5] to move the cursor.
	Enter numbers and text	Position the cursor in the appropriate cell, type in the text or number, and press [Enter] or use a cursor-movement key to put data in a cell.

Table 1.5	Enter formulas and functions	Position the cursor in the appropriate cell, type in a formula or function, and press [Enter] or use a cursor-movement key to put the data in the cell. If you type an invalid formula, Lotus will beep and change the mode indicator to Edit. You must correct the mistake before entering the formula in the cell.
Command Summary (concluded)	Edit a cell	Method One: Position the cursor on the cell that needs to be changed. Retype the contents and then press [Enter].
		Method Two: Position the cursor on the cell that needs to be changed. Press [F2] (Edit). Make your changes to the cell contents that appear in the data entry area, and then press [Enter].
	Use the UNDO command	To see what your spreadsheet looks like when the spreadsheet was last in Ready mode, use the UNDO command by pressing [Alt]+[F4].
	Use Menu mode	Press the slash (/) key to enter Menu mode. To choose an option, highlight it and then press [Enter]. To back out of a command, press [Esc].
	Display Help information	Press [F1] (Help) to display help information about the current command.
	Erasing a Range	Position the cursor at the beginning of the range, /, Range, Erase, highlight the range, [Enter]
	Erasing the Spreadsheet	/, Worksheet, Erase, Yes
	Exit Lotus 1-2-3	/, Quit, Yes, Yes or No, Exit

KEY TERMS

[Alt]   Modifier key on the computer keyboard; when a modifier key is pressed along with another key, the function of that other key is modified. The applications software program determines how modifier keys are used.

[BackSpace]   Used to move the cursor to the left and to simultaneously delete the character to the left.

cell   In a spreadsheet program, this marks the intersection of a column and a row.

cell address   A name that is given to a cell.

[Delete]   Used to delete the character the cursor is positioned on.

[Enter]   Computer keyboard key pressed to execute a command that was entered by typing other keys first.

[Esc]   Most software applications allow the user to press this key to back out of, or cancel, the current command procedure.

formula   In Lotus 1-2-3, a mathematical expression that defines the relationships among various cells in an electronic spreadsheet.

help facility   Most application software packages include a command that enables the user to display helpful information on the screen about a particular topic.

Label mode   Lotus 1-2-3 goes into this mode when an alphabetic character or ', ", or ^ is pressed. Compare **value mode**.

Menu mode   In Lotus 1-2-3, the mode that displays menu options; accessed by pressing the slash (/) key.

period key   In Lotus 1-2-3, this key is used to anchor, or mark, the beginning of a **range**.

range   One or more cells in a spreadsheet that together form a rectangle.

RANGE ERASE   A Lotus 1-2-3 command that enables you to erase a **range** of cells.

Ready mode   In Lotus 1-2-3, the spreadsheet is in this mode when the user can move the cursor from cell to cell.

slash key   Used by Lotus 1-2-3 to invoke **Menu mode**.

UNDO command   Lotus 1-2-3 command that makes it possible to view a spreadsheet as it appeared when it was last in **Ready mode**.

Value mode   Lotus 1-2-3 goes into this mode when a numeric character or +, -, @, $, or (is pressed. Compare **label mode**.

"what-if " analysis   Using Lotus 1-2-3, the ability to change information in the spreadsheet at any time and immediately see the effects of the change on other formulas or calculations.

WORKSHEET ERASE   A Lotus 1-2-3 command that enables you to erase every cell in a spreadsheet.

EXERCISES

SHORT ANSWER

1. What is the procedure for loading Lotus 1-2-3 so that a blank spreadsheet displays?
2. What is a cell?
3. What advantages do electronic spreadsheets have over manual spreadsheets?
4. How do you display Help information on the screen? How do you undo your last command?
5. Describe the different methods for moving the cursor around the spreadsheet.

6. What steps can you take to create consistently reliable spreadsheets?
7. Give some examples of how the keyboard is used in Lotus. (For example, what happens when you press the slash key?)
8. What is the difference between Label mode and Value mode?
9. What is a formula? Provide an example.
10. How do you get into Menu mode? How do you choose a command? Back out of a command?

HANDS-ON

1. In this exercise, you will create the spreadsheet pictured in Figure 1.9.

Figure 1.9

The Fruit
Tracker

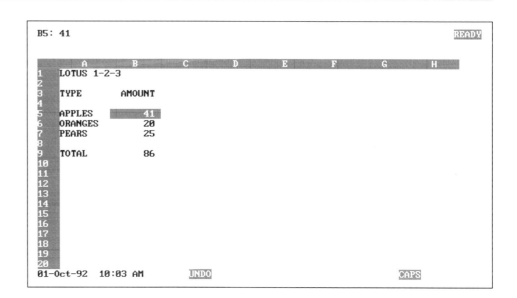

a. Load Lotus 1-2-3 so you can see an empty electronic spreadsheet.
b. Move the cursor to the following cells: (a) A21, (b) A42, (c) A1, (d) J5, (e) J26, (f) A1.
c. Type LOTUS into cell A1.
d. Using the Edit key (F2), edit cell A1 so it contains LOTUS 1-2-3.
e. Position the cursor in the following cells and type the corresponding data:

Move to Cell	TYPE:
A3	TYPE
A5	APPLES
A6	ORANGES
A7	PEARS
A9	TOTAL
(*continued*)	

Move to Cell	TYPE:
B3	"AMOUNT
B5	10
B6	20
B7	25

f.   In cell B9, type a formula that adds the amounts in B5, B6, and B7. After you have done this, the answer 55 should be displaying in cell B9. Now type 41 into cell B5. Note that the formula in cell B9 recalculated the correct answer (86). The screen should look like Figure 1.9.

g.   You don't yet know how to use Lotus's PRINT command (you will use this command in Session 2). For now, to print a copy of your work, hold (Shift) down and press (PrtScr) (Print Screen). Next, press the Online button on your printer and then the Form Feed button to obtain the printed output. (You will have to press the Online button again before you print again.)

2.   To practice using Lotus's menu system and displaying help information, perform the following steps:

a.   Invoke Menu mode.

b.   CHOOSE: Global

c.   CHOOSE: Format

d.   Back out of Menu mode until the mode indicator says READY.

e.   With the spreadsheet in Ready mode, press the Help key ((F1)). Practice moving around in the Help facility. Then exit to Ready mode (using (Esc)).

f.   In Menu mode, highlight the Range option. Press (F1). Note that information about the Range group of commands appears on the screen. When you are finished, exit to Ready mode.

3.   To practice entering text:

a.   Use the WORKSHEET ERASE command to erase any cells that contain data.

b.   Position the cursor in cell C3.

c.   TYPE: ENTERING TEXT

d.   Type ABC into cell C5 so that it is left-aligned.

e.   Type ABC into cell C6 so that it is centered.

f.   Type ABC into cell C7 so that it is right-aligned.

g.   Position the cursor in cell A1. Type your name.

h.   You don't yet know how to use Lotus's PRINT command (you will use this command in Session 2). For now, to print a copy of your work, hold (Shift) down and press (PrtScr) (Print Screen). Next, press the Online button on your printer and then the Form Feed button to obtain the printed output. (You will have to press the Online button again before you print again.)

4. To practice editing and using the UNDO command, perform the following steps (if you're using Lotus 1-2-3, version 2.01, skip to the next exercise):
   a. Use the WORKSHEET ERASE command to erase any cells that contain data.
   b. Type the following data into the corresponding cells:

Move to Cell	TYPE:
A1	TYPE
A2	FOOD
A3	SUPPLIES
A4	LAUNDRY
A5	TOTAL
B1	"AMOUNT
B2	500
B3	250.24
B4	199.57
B5	+B2+B3+B4

   c. Type TEXT into cell B5. Cell B5 no longer contains a formula.
   d. To bring back the formula into cell B9, use the UNDO command. The formula should again be displaying in the cell.
   e. Change the contents of cell B2 to 750. The total in B5 should now be 1199.81.
   f. Change B3 to 243.96. The total should now be 1193.53.

5. To practice erasing ranges, retrieve RANGES from the Advantage Diskette. Perform the tasks listed in column A. When finished, only the instructions in column A will be displaying in the spreadsheet.

6. This exercise produces a spreadsheet to help manage your personal credit card limits and balances. The tasks include entering numbers and editing data.
   a. Use the WORKSHEET ERASE command to erase any cells that contain data.
   b. With your cursor in cell A1:
      TYPE: PERSONAL FINANCIAL PLANNER
      PRESS: (Enter)
   c. Enter the following text labels:

Move to Cell	TYPE:
C3	Budget
D3	Actual
A6	VISA
A7	Chevron
A8	AMEX
A9	M/C

d. Enter the following numbers:

Move to Cell	TYPE:
C6	1200
C7	500
C8	200
C9	75
D6	1200
D7	450
D8	215
D9	135

e. Change the label in cell A6 from "VISA" to "Discover" by typing over the existing entry.
f. Change the label in cell A8 from "AMEX" to "AMEX Gold" using (F2).
g. Change the budgeted value for the Chevron account in cell C7 to 400.
h. Change the actual value for the AMEX Gold card in cell D8 to 210.
i. You don't yet know how to use Lotus's PRINT command (you will use this command in Session 2). For now, to print a copy of your work, hold (Shift) down and press (PrtScr) (Print Screen). Next, press the Online button on your printer and then the Form Feed button to obtain the printed output. (You will have to press the Online button again before you print again.)

7. This exercise provides further practice for entering text, numbers, and formulas.
   a. Use the WORKSHEET ERASE command to erase any cells that contain data.
   b. With your cursor in cell A15:
      TYPE: National Sales Contest
      PRESS: (Enter)
   c. Enter the following text labels:

Move to Cell	TYPE:
C17	Units Sold
A18	Craig
A19	Andrea
A20	Tom
A22	Total Units

d. Enter the following numbers:

Move to Cell	TYPE:
C18	30
C19	55
C20	42

e. Enter a formula to sum the units sold. Place the result of the formula in cell C22.

f. Type your name into cell A13.

g. You don't yet know how to use Lotus's PRINT command (you will use this command in Session 2). For now, to print a copy of your work, hold [Shift] down and press [PrtScr] (Print Screen). Next, press the Online button on your printer and then the Form Feed button to obtain the printed output. (You will have to press the Online button again before you print again.)

LOTUS 1-2-3: WORKING WITH SPREADSHEETS

Spreadsheets may look complicated, but even a new user can begin to construct one in a short period of time. This session shows how to set up a spreadsheet and enter text, numbers, formulas, and functions. Once your spreadsheet is established, you can easily modify it and use it over and over for whatever purpose you designed it for—for example, to produce daily, weekly, or monthly reports.

PREVIEW

When you have completed this session, you will be able to:

Enter labels.
·
Format numbers.
·
Widen columns.
·
Change the current disk and directory.
·
Use the @SUM function.
·
Change numbers.
·
Save and retrieve a spreadsheet.
·
Print a spreadsheet using various Print options.

Why Is This Session Important?
Entering Text (Labels)
Entering Numbers (Values)
The @SUM Function
Formatting Numbers: Currency
Widening Columns
Changing the Current Directory
Saving the Spreadsheet
The SYSTEM Command
Recalculating the Spreadsheet: Changing a Few
   Numbers
Saving the Spreadsheet More Than Once
Retrieving the Spreadsheet
Printing the Spreadsheet
      As-Displayed Format
      Cell-Formulas Format
Print Options
      Using a Settings Sheet (Version 2.2)
      Headers and Footers
      Forcing a Page Break
Summary
      Command Summary
Key Terms
Exercises
      Short Answer
      Hands-On

WHY IS THIS SESSION IMPORTANT?

This session leads you through creating a spreadsheet from start to finish. You will create the spreadsheet in Figure 2.1. This spreadsheet keeps track of monthly expenses (January, February, and March) for the XYZ COMPANY. It maintains a total for each month in row 10 and a total for each type of expense in column E.

Figure 2.1

The completed
QTR1 spreadsheet

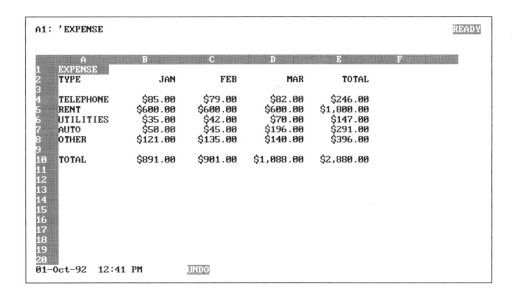

In this session, you will perform the following tasks:

1. Enter the spreadsheet labels; this text serves as the framework for the spreadsheet.

2. Enter the spreadsheet data.

3. Enter the formulas to calculate totals.

4. Use a command to format the numbers in the spreadsheet in the currency (money) format.

5. Use a command to widen columns so you can see all the data in the spreadsheet.

6. Use a command to change the current directory; this tells Lotus where you want to save and retrieve files.

7. Save, retrieve, and print the spreadsheet.

Before proceeding, make sure the following are true:

1. You have loaded Lotus 1-2-3 and are displaying an empty spreadsheet template on the screen.

2. Your Advantage Diskette is inserted in the drive. You will save your work onto the diskette and retrieve the files that have been created for you. (Note: The Advantage Diskette can be made by copying all the files off the instructor's Master Advantage Diskette onto a formatted diskette.)

ENTERING TEXT (LABELS)

Spreadsheet **labels**, or descriptive text, are used to provide a frame of reference for spreadsheet data and formulas. In this section you will enter the labels for the quarterly spreadsheet.

Perform the following steps:

1. In this section you will type the labels into the spreadsheet. So that the letters appear in capitals:
   PRESS: [Caps]
   The message CAPS should appear highlighted in the bottom-right corner of the screen.

2. Make sure the cursor is positioned in cell A1.
   TYPE: EXPENSE
   PRESS: [Enter]
   The text EXPENSE should be in cell A1. If you misspelled EXPENSE, either type it correctly and press [Enter], or use the Edit key ([F2]) (see Session 1). What you have just typed will replace what you had typed previously.

3. PRESS: [↓] *once*
   The cursor should have moved to cell A2.

4. TYPE: TYPE
   PRESS: [Enter]
   The label TYPE should be in cell A2.

5. PRESS: [↓] *twice*
   The cursor should be in cell A4.

6. Position the cursor in the following cells and type in the corresponding labels:

Move to Cell	TYPE:
A4	TELEPHONE
A5	RENT
A6	UTILITIES
A7	AUTO
A8	OTHER
A10	TOTAL

7. In the next few steps you will type the labels (headings) into the range B2..E2. So that the each label will appear on the right side of the cell (lined up above the numbers you will enter in a later step), you will precede each label with a quotation mark ("). (Note: If you omit the quotation mark, the text you type will appear on the left side of the cell; numbers (values), however, always appear on the right side of a cell.) Position the cursor in the following cells and type in the corresponding labels:

Move to Cell	TYPE:
B2	"JAN
C2	"FEB
D2	"MAR
E2	"TOTAL

    All the labels have now been entered into this spreadsheet. The cursor should be positioned in cell E2. Your spreadsheet should now look like Figure 2.2.

Figure 2.2

The text has been entered in the spreadsheet.

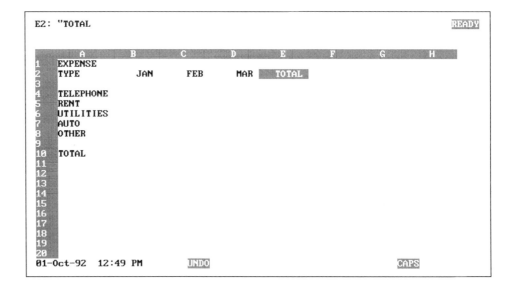

ENTERING NUMBERS (VALUES)

To enter numbers into a Lotus 1-2-3 spreadsheet, you must be in **Value mode**. As described in Session 1, when you type a number or the plus sign, minus sign, open parentheses, period, pound sign, or "at" sign (@), Lotus goes into Value mode and displays VALUE in the upper-right corner of the spreadsheet. Numbers are keyed into cells in the same way text is.

Perform the following steps:

1. Move the cursor to cell B4 so that you can start entering data.

2. In this step you will enter the expense data for January. Position the cursor in the following cells and type in the corresponding number:

Move to Cell	TYPE:
B4	85
B5	600
B6	35
B7	50
B8	121

3. Next you will enter the expense data for February. Position the cursor in the following cells and type in the corresponding number:

Move to Cell	TYPE:
C4	79
C5	600
C6	42
C7	45
C8	135

4. Now enter the expense data for March. Position the cursor in the following cells and type in the corresponding number:

Move to Cell	TYPE:
D4	82
D5	600
D6	70
D7	196
D8	140

All the expense data has now been entered into this spreadsheet. Your spreadsheet should now look like Figure 2.3.

Figure 2.3

The data has been entered in the spread-sheet.

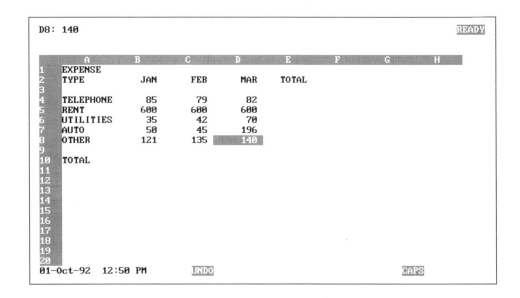

```
D8: 140                                                                    READY

          A          B          C          D          E          F          G          H
1  EXPENSE
2  TYPE        JAN        FEB        MAR       TOTAL
3
4  TELEPHONE    85         79         82
5  RENT        600        600        600
6  UTILITIES    35         42         70
7  AUTO         50         45        196
8  OTHER       121        135        140
9
10 TOTAL
11
12
13
14
15
16
17
18
19
20
01-Oct-92   12:50 PM            UNDO                                      CAPS
```

THE @SUM FUNCTION

An electronic spreadsheet program provides many powerful **functions,** or *electronic shortcuts*, that can be used in formulas. All of Lotus's functions begin with the "at" symbol (@). Functions can save the user a tremendous amount of time. For example, instead of typing

$$+B4+B5+B6+B7+B8$$

to add together the numbers in the range B4..B8, you can use the **@SUM function**. The @SUM function simplifies the process of adding together a range of cells. Using the @SUM function, the formula to add the range B4..B8 would be:

$$@SUM(B4..B8)$$

Imagine the time it would take to write a formula for adding a column of 100 numbers without the @SUM function! With the @SUM function, the user simply specifies the beginning and the end of the range of cells to be added (without spaces), encloses the range in parentheses, and types @SUM before the parentheses. (Additional functions are described in Session 3.)

This spreadsheet will contain a formula in row 10 that adds the five expense amounts you just entered for each month. Also, column E will contain formulas that add the three monthly expense amounts for each expense type (telephone, rent, and so on). Each of these formulas will use the @SUM function.

Perform the following steps:

1. Position the cursor in cell B10 so that a formula can be entered.

2. To add the expenses in column B:
    TYPE: @SUM(B4..B8)
    PRESS: [→]
    The total 891 should be displaying in cell B10. If the correct answer isn't displaying, check to see that you entered the formula correctly (position the cursor on cell B10 and then look at the top-left corner of the screen). If the formula is incorrect, retype it, and then press [Enter]. If your total is wrong but the formula is correct, check to see that the numbers you typed into cells B4, B5, B6, B7, and B8 are the same as in Figure 2.1.

3. Position the cursor in the following cells and type in the corresponding formula:

Move to Cell	TYPE:
C10	@SUM(C4..C8)
D10	@SUM(D4..D8)
E10	@SUM(E4..E8)

    The number 0 should appear in cell E10 because no data is in the cells above. As soon as a formula is entered into one of the cells above E10, a total will appear in cell E10.

4. Position the cursor in the following cells and type in the corresponding formula:

Move to Cell	TYPE:
E4	@SUM(B4..D4)
E5	@SUM(B5..D5)
E6	@SUM(B6..D6)
E7	@SUM(B7..D7)
E8	@SUM(B8..D8)

    All the formulas have now been entered into this spreadsheet (Figure 2.4).

Figure 2.4

The formulas have been entered in the spreadsheet.

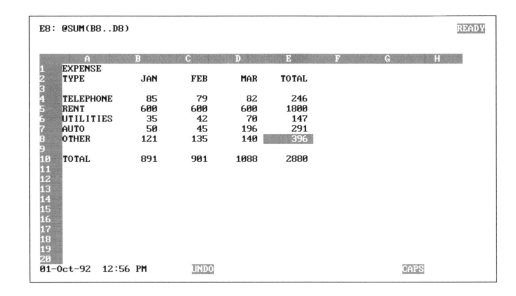

FORMATTING NUMBERS: CURRENCY

Formatting commands allow the user to improve the appearance of a spreadsheet. In this section you are going to change the way the numbers in columns B through E (specifically, the range of cells B4..E10) appear so they are displayed in the currency format with a leading dollar sign and two trailing decimal places. *It is always a good idea to position the cursor in the cell at the beginning of the range you're going to format.*

Perform the following steps to format the range B4..E10 in the currency format:

1. Position the cursor in cell B4 (the beginning of the range you will format).

2. To enter Menu mode:
   TYPE: /

3. CHOOSE: Range, Format, Currency

4. Lotus 1-2-3 is now prompting you to enter the number of decimal places you want the numbers to be formatted to. To accept two decimal places:
   PRESS: [Enter]

5. Lotus 1-2-3 is now prompting you to enter the range of cells you want to format. In this step you will highlight the range to format.
    PRESS: ↓ *until you've highlighted through row 10, and then*
    PRESS: → *until you've highlighted through column E*
    PRESS: Enter

    Don't be alarmed if you see asterisks in a few cells (Figure 2.5). This is Lotus 1-2-3's way of telling you to widen columns because the numbers are too big to fit in the cells. Lotus 1-2-3 won't display a partial number in a cell.

Figure 2.5

Formatted spreadsheet. Columns D and E have to be widened to get rid of the asterisks.

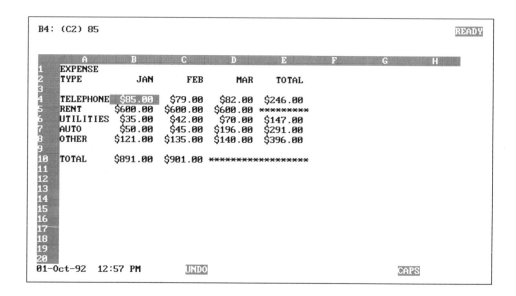

Quick Reference

Formatting a Range of Numbers

1. To initiate Menu mode:
    TYPE: /
2. CHOOSE: Range, Format
3. Choose the option that corresponds to how you want the number to be displayed (Currency, Percent, and so on).
4. Highlight the range to be formatted, and then press Enter.

WIDENING COLUMNS

In this section you will use a command to **widen** the **columns** in the spreadsheet so there is more space between them and so you can see all the numbers in columns D and E. That way you will provide enough space for all the numbers in each cell, and the asterisks will disappear.

Lotus 1-2-3 provides you with a command to widen individual columns in a spreadsheet. To use this command, position the cursor in the column to be widened and then initiate the WORKSHEET COLUMN SET-WIDTH command. Type in a number that represents the new column width and then press (Enter). The number should be equal to or greater than the widest cell contents in the column.

To widen every column in a spreadsheet at once, use theWORKSHEET GLOBAL COLUMN-WIDTH command. *Note: The users of Lotus 1-2-3, version 2.2, can widen a range of columns using the WORKSHEET COLUMN COLUMN-RANGE command.*

In the following steps you will widen all the columns in the spreadsheet using the WORKSHEET GLOBAL COLUMN-WIDTH command. You learn more about global commands in Session 3.

1. When you use a global command, it doesn't matter where the cursor is positioned because every cell in the spreadsheet is affected.

2. To bring up Menu mode:
    TYPE: /

3. CHOOSE: Worksheet, Global, Column-Width

4. Lotus 1-2-3 is now prompting you to enter a column width:
    TYPE: 12
    PRESS: (Enter)
    Every column in the spreadsheet has now been widened to 12 characters and the asterisks have disappeared. Your spreadsheet should look like Figure 2.6.

Figure 2.6

The QTR1 spreadsheet after columns have been widened

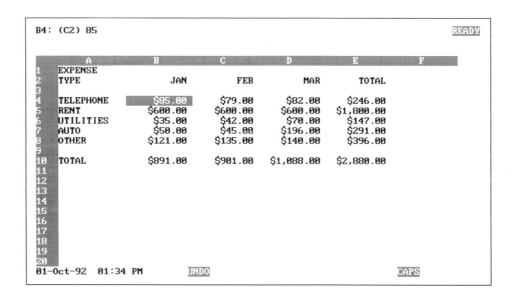

Quick Reference *Widening Every* *Column in the* *Spreadsheet*	1. To initiate Menu mode: TYPE: / 2. CHOOSE: <u>W</u>orksheet, <u>G</u>lobal, <u>C</u>olumn-Width 3. Type in a column width and press (Enter).

Quick Reference *Widening an* *Individual Column*	1. Position the cursor in the column to be widened. 2. To initiate Menu mode: TYPE: / 3. CHOOSE: <u>W</u>orksheet, <u>C</u>olumn, <u>S</u>et-Width 4. Type in a column width and press (Enter).

CHANGING THE CURRENT DIRECTORY

When you load Lotus 1-2-3, it makes an assumption about where it will save your files. (This assumed information, along with other information, is stored in a configuration file on the disk with your Lotus program files.) Lotus typically assumes your files will be saved where the Lotus program files are stored. To change this assumption so that Lotus will always save your files onto the Advantage Diskette in Drive A:, perform the following steps:

1. Put your Advantage Diskette in drive A:.

2. To enter Menu mode:
    TYPE: /

3. CHOOSE: <u>W</u>orksheet, <u>G</u>lobal, <u>D</u>efault, <u>D</u>irectory

4. The name of the current directoy should be listed after the text "Enter default directory:". If A: or A:\ is listed then proceed now to the Saving the Spreadsheet section, otherwise complete the steps in this section.

5. PRESS: (BackSpace) *until the name of the default directoy is erased*

6. To tell Lotus 1-2-3 that your Advantage Diskette is in drive A:
    TYPE: A:
    PRESS: (Enter)

7. To update the configuration file on disk with this new directory setting:
    CHOOSE: <u>U</u>pdate

8. To quit back to Ready mode:
   CHOOSE: Quit

When you save your work, it will automatically be saved onto your Advantage Diskette in drive A:.

Lotus will remember this direction even after you turn off your machine. Therefore, if your diskette will always be in the same diskette drive, you won't have to use this command in subsequent sessions.

....

Quick Reference

Changing the
Default Directory

1. To enter Menu mode:
   TYPE: /
2. CHOOSE: Worksheet, Global, Default, Directory
   PRESS: (BackSpace) *until the name of the default directory is erased*
3. Type the new disk drive designation and press (Enter).
4. To update the configuration file stored on disk:
   CHOOSE: Update
5. To quit back to Ready mode:
   CHOOSE: Quit

....

SAVING THE SPREADSHEET

If you turn the computer off right now or if someone accidentally trips on the power cord to your computer, what do you think would happen? If you guessed you would lose your spreadsheet, you're right. To maintain a permanent copy of your spreadsheet, you should **save** it periodically onto the disk you have designated. Lotus 1-2-3 automatically supplies an extension of WK1 to all your spreadsheet files (some earlier versions of Lotus 1-2-3 supply the extension of WKS). Before saving this spreadsheet you will type your name into cell B1 so that this spreadsheet can be identified as yours when it is printed.

Perform the following steps:

1. Position the cursor in cell B1.

2. TYPE: *your name*
   PRESS: (Enter)

3. Before you save your spreadsheet, it is a good idea (but not required) to move the cursor to cell A1; when you later retrieve the spreadsheet, the cursor will then be in the first cell. First move the cursor to cell A1, and then:
    TYPE: /
    CHOOSE: File, Save

4. Lotus 1-2-3 is now prompting you to type the name you want to assign to the file you're saving.
    TYPE: QTR1
    PRESS: [Enter]

A permanent copy of the spreadsheet you have created has now been saved onto the Advantage Diskette.

....

Quick Reference   1. To initiate Menu mode:
                                 TYPE: /
Saving   2. CHOOSE: File, Save
(for the first time)   3. Type the name (for example, QTR1) you want to assign to the file and then press [Enter].

....

THE SYSTEM COMMAND

If you don't want to exit Lotus 1-2-3 but want to issue a DOS command—for example, to format a diskette onto which you'll save your Lotus files—use the **SYSTEM** command.

To use this command, perform the following steps:

1. To initiate Menu mode:
    TYPE: /
    CHOOSE: System
    Note that the screen has cleared and the system prompt is displaying on the screen. It looks as if you have exited Lotus 1-2-3. In addition, it seems as if you may have lost the worksheet you were working on, but you haven't.

2. If you wanted to issue some DOS commands right now, you would type them in after the DOS prompt and then press [Enter]. To return to the Lotus 1-2-3 display:
    TYPE: exit
    PRESS: [Enter]

CAUTION: Many users accidentally use the SYSTEM command when they are trying to save the spreadsheet. If this happens to you, simply type EXIT and press (Enter) to return to the Lotus 1-2-3 display.

....

Quick Reference

SYSTEM
command

1. To initiate Menu mode:
   TYPE: /
   CHOOSE: <u>S</u>ystem
2. To return to the Lotus 1-2-3 display after using the DOS commands of your choice:
   TYPE: exit
   PRESS: (Enter)

....

RECALCULATING THE SPREADSHEET: CHANGING A FEW NUMBERS

In this step you will change a few numbers in the spreadsheet. As you change them, note how the formulas automatically recalculate the totals when new data is entered. To change a number in a spreadsheet, simply move the cursor to the cell you want to change, retype the contents, and then press (Enter). What you type will replace the old contents.

Perform the following steps:

1. The cursor should be positioned in cell A1. Position the cursor in cell B4.

2. TYPE: 95
   PRESS: (Enter)
   The number 95 should be displaying in cell B4. Note that the formulas in cells B10 and E4 automatically recalculated the correct totals.

3. Position the cursor in cell C6.

4. TYPE: 62
   PRESS: (Enter)
   Cells C10 and E6 now read 921 and 167.

SAVING THE SPREADSHEET MORE THAN ONCE

The procedure to save this updated spreadsheet is almost identical to that previously described; however, you will need to choose one of the following options:

- *Cancel.* By choosing this option, you can save the spreadsheet with a different name.

- *Replace.* By choosing this option, you are replacing the spreadsheet file you previously saved on disk with the updated spreadsheet in RAM. Lotus automatically gives the spreadsheet file the extension of WK1.

- *Backup.* This option saves the updated spreadsheet in RAM onto the disk and gives this file the extension of WK1. In addition, this option gives the previous version (stored on disk) of the spreadsheet the extension of BAK (for "backup").

In this section, you will choose the Replace option.

Perform the following steps:

1. To position the cursor in cell A1 and to then initiate the SAVE command:
   PRESS: [Home]
   TYPE: /
   CHOOSE: File, Save

2. Lotus 1-2-3 is now prompting you to designate the disk drive you want to save the file onto and the name (QTR1) you want to assign to the file. Since Lotus 1-2-3 is assuming you will save it onto the same disk and with the same name as before, simply press [Enter] to accept Lotus 1-2-3's assumption.
   PRESS: [Enter]

3. CHOOSE: Replace

The updated QTR1 file has been saved onto the Advantage Diskette, replacing the old QTR1 file.

....

Quick Reference   1. To initiate Menu mode:
                                 TYPE: /
Saving a Spreadsheet   CHOOSE: File, Save
More Than Once   2. Since Lotus 1-2-3 is assuming you will save the file onto the same disk:
                                 PRESS: [Enter]
                             3. Choose the Replace or Backup option.

....

RETRIEVING THE SPREADSHEET

To **retrieve** a copy of a previously saved spreadsheet file from the disk so you can work with it, use the FILE RETRIEVE command. In this section you will first erase the data from your screen and then retrieve the QTR1 file from your Advantage Diskette.

CAUTION: If spreadsheet data is displaying on your screen when you retrieve a file from disk, the retrieved spreadsheet will replace what was previously displaying on the screen. Therefore, make sure to save your work before retrieving a spreadsheet file.

Perform the following steps to erase the spreadsheet area. (The WORKSHEET ERASE command was described in Session 1.)

1. To enter Menu mode:
    TYPE: /

2. CHOOSE: Worksheet, Erase, Yes

Your screen should look like it did when you first loaded Lotus.

To retrieve the QTR1 file from the Advantage Diskette, perform the following steps:

1. To enter Menu mode:
    TYPE: /

2. CHOOSE: File, Retrieve

3. An incomplete list of files should be displaying on the second line; the rest of the files are off the right side of the screen window. Press ⟶ until the cursor is highlighting QTR1.

4. If the cursor is highlighting the QTR1 file:
    PRESS: Enter

The data stored in the QTR1 file should be displaying on the screen.

....

Quick Reference   1. To enter Menu mode:
                            TYPE: /

Retrieving   2. CHOOSE: File, Retrieve
                       3. Highlight the file you want to retrieve and press Enter.

....

PRINTING THE SPREADSHEET

You have the option of printing a spreadsheet in one of two forms: as a report or as a list of specifications. In Lotus 1-2-3, the report form is called the **as-displayed format,** which is what you see on the screen. To see what formulas you have in each cell of the spreadsheet and how each cell is formatted, you need to use the specifications form. In Lotus 1-2-3, this form is called the **cell-formulas format.** It's a good idea to print out a cell-formulas format for every spreadsheet you create, so that you can recreate the spreadsheet's specifications (formulas) if the spreadsheet is accidentally erased off the disk.

Lotus 1-2-3 makes certain assumptions about your printed spreadsheet. For example, it assumes your spreadsheet will print with a left margin of 4 (characters) and a right margin of 76. We lead you through changing some of these assumptions, or default settings, in the next section. For now, you will print the spreadsheet in both the as-displayed and cell-formulas formats without changing any assumptions that Lotus 1-2-3 makes. Before initiating the **PRINT** command, make sure your computer is attached to a printer (that contains paper) and that the printer is on. Printing the spreadsheet involves specifying the range of cells (A1..E10) to be printed.

AS-DISPLAYED FORMAT

Perform the following steps to print the spreadsheet in the as-displayed format:

1. To enter Menu mode:
    TYPE: /
    CHOOSE: Print

2. Lotus now wants to know whether to direct the output of the PRINT command to a file or to the printer. You will choose the Printer option.
    CHOOSE: Printer

3. Some additional options should appear on the top of the screen. You will choose the Range option.
    CHOOSE: Range

4. Lotus 1-2-3 is now waiting for you to specify the range of cells to print.
    TYPE: A1..E10
    PRESS: (Enter)

5. CHOOSE: Options, Other, As-Displayed

6. To move up one level in the print hierarchy:
    PRESS: (Esc)

7. Before printing the spreadsheet, choose the Align option so that Lotus knows where the top of the page is. After choosing this option, Lotus knows to space down a few lines before printing your spreadsheet (for a top margin) and shouldn't print your spreadsheet over the paper's perforation (if you are using continuous-form paper).
CHOOSE: Align

8. To print:
CHOOSE: Go
The spreadsheet should be printing out on the printer.

9. If you are using continuous-form paper, to move the paper up until the next perforation after your spreadsheet is printed:
CHOOSE: Page

10. To exit the PRINT command:
CHOOSE: Quit

....

Quick Reference   1. To enter Menu mode:
                                 TYPE: /
Printing   2. CHOOSE: Print, Printer, Range
(As-Displayed)   3. Type in the range of cells you want to print and press [Enter].
                             4. CHOOSE: Options, Other, As-Displayed
                             5. To move up one level in the print hierarchy:
                                 PRESS: [Esc]
                             6. CHOOSE: Align, Go, Page, Quit

....

Cell-Formulas Format

Perform the following steps to print the spreadsheet in the cell-formulas format:

1. To enter Menu mode:
TYPE: /
CHOOSE: Print, Printer

2. The Range option is highlighted. However, since you already specified the range of cells to print, you don't need to specify it again. Ordinarily you would type in the range.) To tell Lotus 1-2-3 you want to print in the cell-formulas format:
CHOOSE: Options, Other, Cell-formulas

3. To move up one level so that you can access the GO command:
PRESS: [Esc]

4. Before actually printing the spreadsheet, choose the Align option to tell Lotus where the top of the page is:
    CHOOSE: Align

5. To print:
    CHOOSE: Go
    The spreadsheet should be printing out on the printer. The printout should look like Figure 2.7.

Figure 2.7

Cell-formulas
printout of the
QTR1 spread-
sheet

```
A1:  'EXPENSE
B1:  '(your name)
A2:  'TYPE
B2:  "JAN
C2:  "FEB
D2:  "MAR
E2:  "TOTAL
A4:  'TELEPHONE
B4:  (C2) 95
C4:  (C2) 79
D4:  (C2) 82
E4:  (C2) @SUM(B4..D4)
A5:  'RENT
B5:  (C2) 600
C5:  (C2) 600
D5:  (C2) 600
E5:  (C2) @SUM(B5..D5)
A6:  'UTILITIES
B6:  (C2) 35
C6:  (C2) 62
D6:  (C2) 70
E6:  (C2) @SUM(B6..D6)
A7:  'AUTO
B7:  (C2) 50
C7:  (C2) 45
D7:  (C2) 196
E7:  (C2) @SUM(B7..D7)
A8:  'OTHER
B8:  (C2) 121
C8:  (C2) 135
D8:  (C2) 140
E8:  (C2) @SUM(B8..D8)
A10: 'TOTAL
B10: (C2) @SUM(B4..B8)
C10: (C2) @SUM(C4..C8)
D10: (C2) @SUM(D4..D8)
E10: (C2) @SUM(E4..E8)
```

6. If you are using a printer with continuous-form paper, to move the paper up to the next perforation:
    CHOOSE: Page

7. To exit the PRINT command:
    CHOOSE: Quit

8. At this point, it would be a good idea to save the QTR1 spreadsheet again, because Lotus saves with the file the print range you specified.

....

Quick Reference

Printing
(Cell-Formulas)

1. To enter Menu mode:
    TYPE: /
2. CHOOSE: Print, Printer, Range
3. Type in the range of cells you want to print and press Enter.
4. CHOOSE: Options, Other, Cell-formulas
5. To move up one level in the print hierarchy:
    PRESS: Esc
6. CHOOSE: Align, Go, Page, Quit

....

PRINT OPTIONS

When you print a spreadsheet, Lotus assumes the following:

-   Left Margin: 4 spaces from the left side of the page

-   Right Margin: 76 spaces from the left side of the page, which leaves 4 spaces on the right side of the page

-   Top Margin: 2 lines from the top of the page

-   Bottom Margin: 2 lines from the bottom of the page

-   Page Length: 66 lines

You can change any of these assumptions by selecting the OPTIONS command in the Print menu. Table 2.1 describes Lotus's print options.

Table 2.1	Option	Description
Description of Lotus 1-2-3's print options	Borders	Prints descriptive information (such as headings) from specific rows and columns in your spreadsheet to the left and top of every page of print output. Borders are often used as a frame of reference for spreadsheets that are longer than a page.
	Footer	Prints a line of text just above the bottom margin of every page. Lotus 1-2-3 automatically leaves two blank lines above the footer.
	Header	Prints a line of text just above the top margin of every page. Lotus 1-2-3 automatically leaves two blank lines below the header.
	Margins	Sets the left, right, top, and bottom margins, or clears all margins. This command is useful if you need to print your spreadsheet on paper that is larger or smaller than 8 1/2" by 11".
	Other	Determines whether your spreadsheet is printed in the as-displayed or cell-formulas format, or whether headers, footers, and page breaks are included in your spreadsheet.
	Pg-Length	Sets the number of lines to be included on the printed page.
	Quit	Exits you to the Print menu.
	Setup	Enables you to control your printer by sending special codes to it in the form of a setup string. For example, depending on the type of printer you're using, you can send a setup string to your printer that will cause it to print in landscape mode (from the top of the page to the bottom rather than from the left to right).

In this section you will practice printing the INCOME spreadsheet (stored on your Advantage Diskette) using a few different print commands. You will:

1. Use the header and footer options. A header will print on the top of every page of your printout. A footer will print on the bottom of every page of the printout.

2. Force a page break so that certain rows of a spreadsheet print on one page and others print on the next page.

But first we'd like to describe what settings sheets are.

USING A SETTINGS SHEET (VERSION 2.2)

(Note: If you are using Lotus 1-2-3, version 2.01, proceed to the Headers and Footers section.) Because Lotus 1-2-3 has so many print options, you may not be able to remember the ones you have used. For this reason, Lotus 1-2-3 2.2 provides you with a way to view the current Print settings. The screen that shows you these settings is referred to as a **settings sheet.**

When you're in the Print menu, by pressing F6 (Window), you can display all the current Print settings (Figure 2.8). You can return to the spreadsheet by pressing F6 again. You can view the print settings sheet to see what your current print settings are. If you want to change them, you choose various options. You can double-check the changes by viewing the print settings sheet again.

Figure 2.8

Print settings
sheet

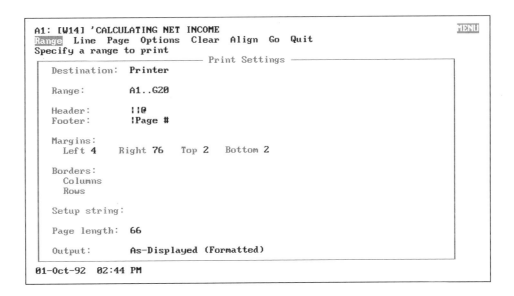

Quick Reference
Using a Settings Sheet
When using a PRINT command, if the settings sheet isn't displaying, press F6 to display the print settings sheet. Pressing F6 again allows you to return to the spreadsheet.

HEADERS AND FOOTERS

If your spreadsheet prints on more than one page, you may want to include page numbers in a header that prints on the top of every page or a footer that prints on the bottom of every page. Or you may want to include text in a header or footer that identifies the spreadsheet.

If you want the header or footer to appear centered, you must preface the header or footer information with |. (Note: The | symbol is located on the same key as the backslash). Similarly, if you want the header or footer to appear against the right margin, you must preface the header or footer information with two | symbols. If you include @ in a header or footer, the current date will print. If you include # in a header or footer, the current page number will print. In the steps below you will specify a header that prints the current date against the right margin (||@) and a footer that prints a centered page number (|Page #). (Figure 2.8 shows the settings sheet with these defined header and footer specifications.)

Perform the following steps to print a header and a footer:

1. Exit from the QTR1 spreadsheet and retrieve INCOME from the Advantage Diskette.

2. To enter Menu mode:
   TYPE: /

3. CHOOSE: Print, Printer, Range

4. To specify the range of cells to print:
   TYPE: A1..G20
   PRESS: (Enter)

5. CHOOSE: Options, Header

6. To include the current date against the right margin in a header:
   TYPE: | | @
   PRESS: (Enter)
   The print settings sheet now displays || next to "Header:".

7. To include a centered page number in a footer:
   CHOOSE: Footer
   TYPE: |Page #
   PRESS: (Enter)

8. To move up one level in the print hierarchy so you can access the GO command:
   PRESS: (Esc)

9. Before choosing the Go option, choose the Align option to tell Lotus where the top of the page is:
   CHOOSE: Align, Go
   The spreadsheet should print out on the printer.

10. If you are using a printer with continuous-form paper, to move the paper to the next perforation, and then quit the Print menu:
    CHOOSE: Page, Quit

1. To initiate Menu mode:
    TYPE: /
2. CHOOSE: <u>P</u>rint, <u>P</u>rinter, <u>O</u>ptions
3. Choose the Header or Footer option.
4. Type in the header or footer information.
5. To move up one level in the print hierarchy so you can access the GO command:
    PRESS: [Esc]
6. CHOOSE: <u>A</u>lign, <u>G</u>o, <u>P</u>age, <u>Q</u>uit

FORCING A PAGE BREAK

To force a page break in your spreadsheet, use the **WORKSHEET PAGE** command. This command forces a page break where the command is entered. Once the command has been used, a blank line appears in the spreadsheet, and :: displays at the position of the cursor. The :: tells Lotus to begin printing on a new page at this point. If you decide at a later time to delete a page break, you must use the **WORKSHEET DELETE ROW** command.

Pretend that the INCOME spreadsheet contains over 30 rows of information. You want to print the first 10 rows on the first page and the next 20 rows on the second page. To practice the use of the WORKSHEET PAGE command, you will insert a page break in the middle of the INCOME spreadsheet.

Perform the following steps:

1. The INCOME spreadsheet should be visible on the screen. Position the cursor in cell A10.

2. TYPE: /
    CHOOSE: <u>W</u>orksheet, <u>P</u>age
    The screen should look like Figure 2.9.

3. Print the spreadsheet in the as-displayed format. Note that the first few expense amounts print on page one and the rest of the spreadsheet prints on page two.

4. To delete the page break code, position the cursor in cell A10 and then do the following:.
    TYPE: /
    CHOOSE: <u>W</u>orksheet, <u>D</u>elete, <u>R</u>ow
    PRESS: [Enter]

Figure 2.9

A page break has been inserted in the middle of the INCOME spreadsheet.

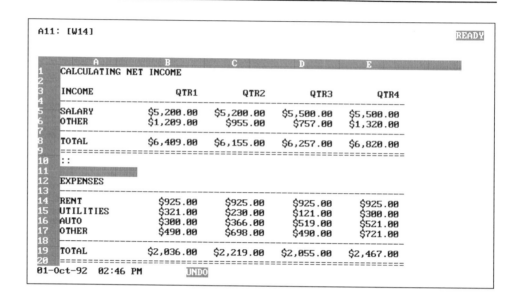

5. Save your spreadsheet and then exit Lotus (unless you're proceeding with the Hands-On exercises).

Quick Reference

Forcing a Page Break

1. Position the cursor in the row where you want the page break to occur.
2. TYPE: /
    CHOOSE: Worksheet, Page

Quick Reference

Deleting a Page Break

1. Position the cursor in the row where the page break occurs.
2. TYPE: /
    CHOOSE: Worksheet, Delete, Row

SUMMARY

The tasks you performed in this lesson are essential in spreadsheet development. Entering spreadsheet labels forms the framework for the spreadsheet, which starts to fill in as you enter data. By using formulas you can mathematically manipulate ranges of numbers. This session used the @SUM function to total up ranges of numbers.

An important step is saving your work onto disk using the FILE SAVE command so that you can retrieve and use the spreadsheet later. When you make changes to a spreadsheet file and then save the file again, you will replace the file on the disk with the updated contents of the spreadsheet in RAM.

To print the spreadsheet you define, or highlight, the print range; in other words you must tell Lotus what cells you want to print. In addition, you may want to include some special features in your printouts, such as a header or a footer, by using the OPTIONS command in the Print menu. Once you print the spreadsheet, it's a good idea to then save the spreadsheet again so that the specifications you defined in the Print menu (such as the spreadsheet range) are saved along with your file.

If you want to review the print settings you are using, you can use F6 (version 2.2) to bring up the print settings screen. When you change settings using the options in the Print menu, the changes will be displayed in the print settings screen.

COMMAND SUMMARY

The following table provides a list of the commands and procedures covered in this session.

Table 2.2	Format a range of numbers	/, Range, Format, choose a formatting option, (Enter), highlight the range of cells to be formatted, (Enter)
Command Summary	Widen an individual column	Position the cursor in the column to be widened, /, Worksheet, Column, Set, type in the new column width, (Enter)
	Widen a range of columns	Position the cursor in the first column of the range to be widened, /, Worksheet, Column, Column-Range, Set-Width, highlight the range of columns to be widened, (Enter), type in a new column width, (Enter)
	Widen every column	/, Worksheet, Global, Column-width, type in a new column width, (Enter)
	Change the current directory (temporary change)	/, File, Directory, type in the new disk drive designation, (Enter)

Table 2.2 Command Summary (concluded)	Change the current directory (change recorded in the Lotus setup file)	/, <u>W</u>orksheet, <u>G</u>lobal, <u>D</u>efault, <u>D</u>irectory, type in the new disk drive designation, (Enter), <u>U</u>pdate, <u>Q</u>uit
	Save (for the first time)	/, <u>F</u>ile, <u>S</u>ave, type the spreadsheet name, (Enter)
	Save (more than once)	/, <u>F</u>ile, <u>S</u>ave, type the spreadsheet name, (Enter), <u>R</u>eplace
	Use a DOS command without exiting Lotus	/, <u>S</u>ystem, to return to Lotus, type exit, (Enter)
	Retrieve a spreadsheet	/ <u>F</u>ile, <u>R</u>etrieve, type the spreadsheet name or highlight it, (Enter)
	Print (as-displayed)	/, <u>P</u>rint, <u>P</u>rinter, <u>R</u>ange, type or highlight the range to be printed, (Enter), <u>O</u>ptions, <u>O</u>ther, <u>A</u>s-displayed, (Esc), <u>A</u>lign, <u>G</u>o, <u>P</u>age, <u>Q</u>uit
	Print (cell-formulas)	/, <u>P</u>rint, <u>P</u>rinter, <u>R</u>ange, type or highlight the range to be printed, (Enter), <u>O</u>ptions, <u>O</u>ther, <u>C</u>ell-formulas, (Esc), <u>A</u>lign, <u>G</u>o, <u>P</u>age, <u>Q</u>uit
	Print a header/footer	/, <u>P</u>rint, <u>P</u>rinter, <u>R</u>ange, type or highlight the range to be printed, (Enter), <u>O</u>ptions, <u>H</u>eader/<u>F</u>ooter, type in the header/footer information, (Enter), (Esc), <u>A</u>lign, <u>G</u>o, <u>P</u>age, <u>Q</u>uit
	Force a page break	Position the cursor in the row where you want the page break to occur, /, <u>W</u>orksheet, <u>P</u>age
	Delete a forced page break	Position the cursor in the row where the page break occurs, /, <u>W</u>orksheet, <u>D</u>elete, <u>R</u>ow

KEY TERMS

as-displayed format   In Lotus 1-2-3, choosing this format enables the user to print the report as it is displayed on the screen. Compare **cell-formulas format**.

cell-formulas format   In Lotus 1-2-3, this format enables the user to print the characteristics of every cell in the spreadsheet. Compare **as-displayed format**.

formatting commands In electronic spreadsheet processing, the alteration of numbers by the addition of dollar signs, percent signs, decimal places, and so on.

function In Lotus 1-2-3, mathematical shortcuts that can be used in formulas to perform calculations. All of Lotus's functions begin with @.

Label mode Lotus 1-2-3 goes into this mode when an alphabetic character or ', ", or ^ is pressed. Compare **Value mode**.

PRINT A Lotus 1-2-3 command that enables you to print a spreadsheet in the **as-displayed** or **cell-formulas** format.

retrieve A process that enables the user to bring into RAM a copy of a file that is stored on disk.

save Activity of permanently storing data from a microcomputer's RAM (main memory) on disk.

settings sheet Status screens in Lotus 1-2-3 that show all the current spreadsheet settings.

@SUM function Lotus 1-2-3 function used to determine the total amount of values stored in a range of spreadsheet cells.

SYSTEM Lotus 1-2-3 command that enables you to use DOS (disk operating system) commands without exiting Lotus.

Value mode Lotus 1-2-3 goes into this mode when a numeric characer or +, -, @, $, or (is pressed. Compare **Label mode**.

widen columns In Lotus 1-2-3, columns often need to be widened in order to display the data in the column. Unless changed, a column is nine characters wide.

WORKSHEET DELETE ROW A Lotus 1-2-3 command that enables you to delete a row in a spreadsheet.

WORKSHEET PAGE A Lotus 1-2-3 command that enables you to insert a page break in a spreadsheet. Whatever follows the page break will print beginning at the top of the next page.

EXERCISES

SHORT ANSWER

1. What do you have to do if a number is too wide to fit in a cell?
2. If you type the number 5 into cell A3, but later decide you want the number 15 in cell A3, what must you do?
3. What is the purpose of changing the current directory?
4. What is the difference between as-displayed and cell-formulas printouts?
5. Why is it important to save your spreadsheet before exiting Lotus?
6. What is a range?
7. What does Lotus 1-2-3 always ask you when you save a spreadsheet more than once?

8. What can you do to numbers to change the way they display—that is, reformat them—in the spreadsheet?
9. Cells A4 and A5 contain numbers. Using the @SUM function, what would you type into cell A6 to add the two numbers?
10. Describe the procedure for getting your name to appear in cell A1.

HANDS-ON

1. In this exercise you will practice entering text and numbers, and using the @SUM function in a spreadsheet that keeps track of the number of employees in the Widget Corporation. In addition, you will save, retrieve, and then edit the spreadsheet. Perform the following steps:
   a. Enter the following headings into the appropriate cells:

Move to Cell	TYPE:
A1	EMPLOYEES
A2	WIDGET CORPORATION
C3	1991
D3	1992
E3	1993
B4	Boston
B5	Chicago
B6	Houston
B7	Seattle
B9	TOTAL

   b. Enter the following data into the appropriate cells:

Move to Cell	TYPE:
C4	244
C5	132
C6	122
C7	94
D4	180
D5	62
D6	145
D7	120
E4	175
E5	60
E6	145
E7	118

   c. Use the @SUM function in C9..E9 to add together the four amounts above.
   d. Save the spreadsheet as WIDGET on your Advantage Diskette.
   e. Clear the spreadsheet area using the WORKSHEET ERASE command.

    f.   Retrieve WIDGET from Advantage Diskette.

    g.   Edit the spreadsheet by moving to the appropriate cells and typing in the corresponding data:

Move to Cell	TYPE:
C5	102
C7	91
D4	38
D5	65
E6	149
E7	123

    h.   Save (and replace) WIDGET on the Advantage Diskette.

2. To practice retrieving a file, editing it, and then saving it under a different name, perform the following steps:

    a.   Retrieve QTR1-EX from the Advantage Diskette.

    b.   Edit QTR1-EX (by changing the cells listed below) to reflect the second quarter's expenses. Remember that you can simply position the cursor on the cell you want to edit and retype the contents.

Move to Cell	TYPE:
B2	"APR
C2	"MAY
D2	"JUNE
B6	43.44
C4	39.65
C7	119
D6	83.91
D8	98.60

    c.   Include your name in cell B1.

    d.   Save this spreadsheet onto the Advantage Diskette as QTR2-EX. Note: When prompted for a file name, type QTR2-EX to replace the existing name.

    e.   Print the spreadsheet in both the as-displayed and cell-formulas formats.

3. Retrieve INCOME92 from the Advantage Diskette. Do the following:

    a.   Widen column A so all the text is visible in cells A7 and A8.

    b.   Type your name into cell C3.

    c.   Type formulas into the four cells in row 10 that subtract the EXPENSES amount from the GROSS RECEIPTS amount in the cells above. Hint: Use the dash (-) to represent the minus sign.

    d.   Type formulas into cells F7, F8, and F10 that add the four amounts to the left—these three formulas should use the @SUM function.

    e. Format all the cells that contain numbers in the currency format to two decimal places. *If necessary, widen columns to accommodate the numbers.*

    f. Save this spreadsheet onto the Advantage Diskette as INCOME92. (Note: Choose Replace.)

    g. Print this spreadsheet in both the as-displayed and cell-formulas formats.

4. Retrieve BUDGET from the Advantage Diskette. Perform the following steps:
    a. Type your name into cell C2.
    b. Use the RANGE FORMAT command to format all the numbers in the spreadsheet in the Currency format to two decimals. *If necessary, widen columns to accommodate the numbers.*
    c. Enter @SUM formulas into column F to add the four amounts to the left. For example, enter a formula into cell F6 to add the four weekly sales amounts.
    d. Type @SUM formulas into the range B17..F17 to add the four expense amounts above.
    e. Type formulas into the range B19..F19 that calculate NET PROFIT by subtracting the TOTAL EXPENSES amount from the GROSS PROFIT amount.
    f. Save this file onto the Advantage Diskette as BUDGET.
    g. Print the BUDGET spreadsheet in both the as-displayed and cell-formulas formats.

5. Create a spreadsheet that you can use for the month of January to keep track of your weekly expenses and available cash. Make sure to do the following:
    a. Clear your screen using the WORKSHEET ERASE command. (Note: Choose Yes.)
    b. Type in labels for the spreadsheet.
    c. Calculate a column total for each type of expense.
    d. Calculate the difference between cash and expenses. The difference might be called EXTRA CASH or CASH FLOW.
    e. Type JANUARY into cell A1 and type your name into cell C1.
    f. Decide how to best set up this spreadsheet. (However, make sure to satisfy all the preceding requirements.)
    g. Save the spreadsheet onto the Advantage Diskette as JAN.
    h. Print the spreadsheet in both the as-displayed and cell-formulas formats.
    i. Edit the JAN spreadsheet to reflect February's expenses by changing some of the amounts. Save the updated spreadsheet onto the Advantage Diskette as FEB. Print the spreadsheet in the as-displayed format.

6. To practice using the UNDO command, perform the following steps:
   a. Retrieve QTR1-EX from the Advantage Data Diskette.
   b. Clear RAM using the WORKSHEET ERASE command.
   c. Use the UNDO command ([Alt]+[F4]). Note that the QTR1-EX spreadsheet appears on the screen. Use the UNDO command again. The screen should be clear. Use the UNDO command one more time to display the QTR1-EX spreadsheet.
   d. Retrieve the BUDGET file from the Advantage Diskette. Use the UNDO command to display the QTR1-EX spreadsheet. Use the UNDO command to again display the BUDGET spreadsheet.
   e. Exit both files.

SESSION 3

LOTUS 1-2-3:
ADDITIONAL SPREADSHEET PROCEDURES

Electronic spreadsheets are themselves time savers compared to the old pencil-and-paper spreadsheets. Now let us demonstrate some time savers for the time saver. Instead of entering in the contents of every cell individually, as was done in the last session, you can use some command shortcuts that work with ranges of cells. You can also use some functions that are built into the program, which provide you with powerful problem-solving capabilities.

PREVIEW

When you have completed this session, you will be able to:

Create an underline.
·
Use the COPY command.
·
Use the MOVE command.
·
Use global and range formatting commands.
·
Use the @AVG, @MIN, and @MAX functions.
·
Use the @IF and @DATE functions.
·
Describe what circular references are and how to avoid them.

SESSION OUTLINE

Why Is This Session Important?
Copying
 Copying Labels: Creating Underlines
 Copying Formulas
Moving
Formatting Commands
 Global Commands: Formatting Numbers
  and Widening Columns
 Range Commands: Formatting Numbers
  and Realigning Labels
@AVG
@MIN
@MAX
@DATE
 Calculating with Dates
@IF
Circular References: Avoid Them
Summary
 Command Summary
Key Terms
Exercises
 Short Answer
 Hands-On

WHY IS THIS SESSION IMPORTANT?

In this session you learn how to perform additional spreadsheet procedures, including copying, formatting, and using functions. You will use these procedures in almost every spreadsheet you create. To practice these commands, you'll use the NET-INC spreadsheet (Figure 3.1) stored on the Advantage Diskette. In its current form, this spreadsheet doesn't contain any underlines or formulas. You will enter them and then practice copying them. Next you will format the spreadsheet so that certain cells appear in the currency format and others appear in the percent format. When you finish formatting, the spreadsheet will look like Figure 3.2 (part of the spreadsheet has scrolled off the screen to the right). In addition, you will insert functions in this spreadsheet to calculate income statistics. You will then use the BILLS spreadsheet, also stored on the Advantage Diskette, to learn how to use the @DATE and @IF functions.

Figure 3.1

The NET-INC spreadsheet without underlines or formulas

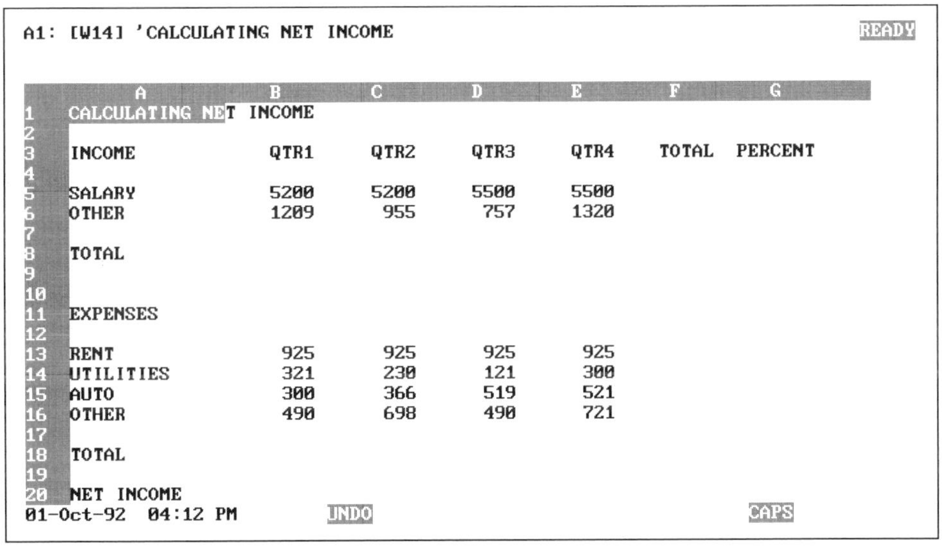

```
A1: [W14] 'CALCULATING NET INCOME                                    READY

            A            B        C        D        E      F        G
 1   CALCULATING NET INCOME
 2
 3   INCOME          QTR1     QTR2     QTR3     QTR4   TOTAL   PERCENT
 4
 5   SALARY          5200     5200     5500     5500
 6   OTHER           1209      955      757     1320
 7
 8   TOTAL
 9
10
11   EXPENSES
12
13   RENT             925      925      925      925
14   UTILITIES        321      230      121      300
15   AUTO             300      366      519      521
16   OTHER            490      698      490      721
17
18   TOTAL
19
20   NET INCOME
01-Oct-92  04:12 PM            UNDO                           CAPS
```

Before proceeding, make sure the following are true:

1. You have loaded Lotus 1-2-3 and are displaying an empty spreadsheet template on the screen.

2. Your Advantage Diskette is inserted in the drive. You will save your work onto the diskette and retrieve the files that have been created for you. (Note: The Advantage Diskette can be made by copying all the files off the instructor's Master Advantage Diskette onto a formatted diskette.)

Figure 3.2

The NET-INC
spreadsheet
after it has been
formatted. (Part
of the spread-
sheet has scrolled
of the screen to
the right.)

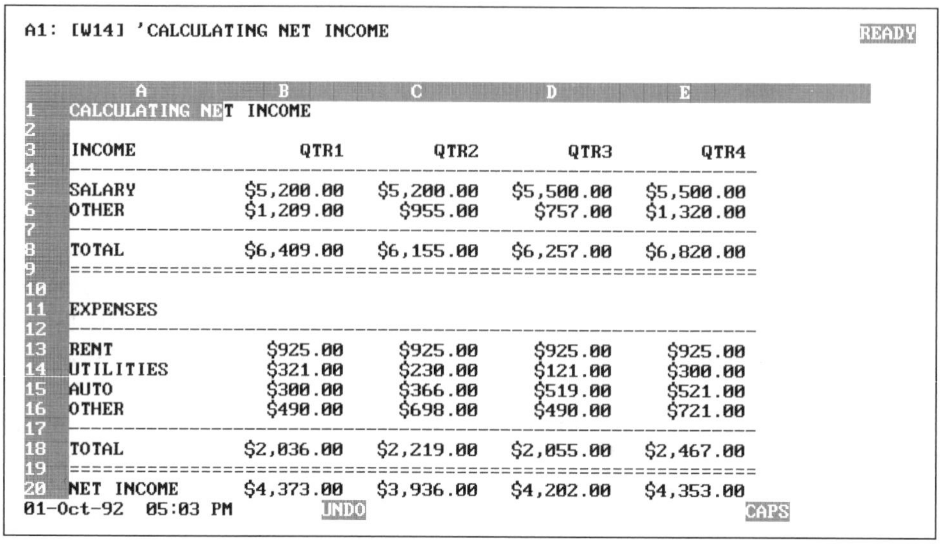

```
A1: [W14] 'CALCULATING NET INCOME                                    READY

           A              B           C           D           E
 1  CALCULATING NET INCOME
 2
 3  INCOME              QTR1        QTR2        QTR3        QTR4
 4  ----------------------------------------------------------------
 5  SALARY            $5,200.00   $5,200.00   $5,500.00   $5,500.00
 6  OTHER             $1,209.00     $955.00     $757.00   $1,320.00
 7  ----------------------------------------------------------------
 8  TOTAL             $6,409.00   $6,155.00   $6,257.00   $6,820.00
 9  ================================================================
10
11  EXPENSES
12  ----------------------------------------------------------------
13  RENT                $925.00     $925.00     $925.00     $925.00
14  UTILITIES           $321.00     $230.00     $121.00     $300.00
15  AUTO                $300.00     $366.00     $519.00     $521.00
16  OTHER               $490.00     $698.00     $490.00     $721.00
17  ----------------------------------------------------------------
18  TOTAL             $2,036.00   $2,219.00   $2,055.00   $2,467.00
19  ================================================================
20  NET INCOME        $4,373.00   $3,936.00   $4,202.00   $4,353.00
01-Oct-92  05:03 PM          UNDO                            CAPS
```

COPYING

The contents of a cell can be quite long. What happens if you want to repeat a text string that is 30 characters long in 25 places in the spreadsheet? Do you have to key in 750 characters? No. Lotus enables you to copy text, numbers, and formulas from one cell (or a range of cells) into another range of cells. Generally speaking, the steps for copying include:

1. Initiate the COPY command.

2. Tell Lotus what cell or range of cells you want to copy from.

3. Tell Lotus what cell or range of cells you want to copy to.

When a formula is copied into one or more cells, the spreadsheet program analyzes the cell from which the formula is being copied and the cell(s) the formula is being copied to. It then adjusts the cell references in the copied formulas to reflect their new locations in the spreadsheet. This adjustment spares the user from typing many formulas (that essentially do the same thing, such as adding a range of cells) into the spreadsheet and thus saves the user a tremendous amount of time. A cell reference that adjusts when it is copied is referred to as a **relative cell reference.** There are times when you don't want a cell reference to adjust when copied. In other words, you want the formula to contain an **absolute cell reference.** In this session, we describe when relative and absolute cell references are used in formulas.

COPYING LABELS: CREATING UNDERLINES

The time it takes to create a spreadsheet is reduced if users use the **COPY** command to copy text or labels that appear repeatedly in a spreadsheet. A common application for copying text or labels occurs when you are creating an underline. To enter an underline using Lotus 1-2-3, you first fill a cell with dashes to mark where you want the underline to begin. Then you copy the dashes into the other cells in which you want the underline to appear. To fill a cell with dashes, Lotus 1-2-3 uses the **BACKSLASH-FILL** command. *The advantage of entering underlines using the BACKSLASH-FILL command (rather than simply typing in a series of dashes) is that when you widen a column, the underline automatically widens with the column.*

In this section you will retrieve the file named NET-INC from the Advantage Diskette and then create underlines in rows 4, 7, 9, 12, 17, and 19.

Perform the following steps:

1. Retrieve the file named NET-INC from the Advantage Diskette using the FILE RETRIEVE command. (If you've forgotten how to use this command, refer to Session 2.)

2. The NET-INC spreadsheet should be displaying on the screen.

Perform the following steps to create underlines in this spreadsheet:

1. These next few steps will lead you through putting an underline into row 4. Position the cursor in cell A4.
   TYPE: \-
   PRESS: (Enter)
   Cell A4 should now be filled with dashes. *If you want a row to be filled with a double line then type an equal sign after the backslash (=).*

2. The cursor should still be positioned on cell A4. Bring up Menu mode to copy the dashes into cells B4 through G4:
   TYPE: /
   CHOOSE: Copy

3. Lotus is now prompting you to enter the cell range you are copying from. Lotus assumes you are copying from the cell the cursor is positioned on. Since this is a correct assumption:
   PRESS: (Enter)

4. Lotus is now waiting for you to specify the range of cells you are copying to. In this step you will copy the dashes into the range A4 through G4 (it doesn't matter if a copy of cell A4 is made onto cell A4). To tell Lotus you are

copying into more than one cell, you must anchor in place the reference to cell A4 by pressing the period key (.).
TYPE: .
PRESS: [→] *until the range A4..G4 is highlighted*
PRESS: [Enter]
Underlines should be displaying in row 4. If they're not, repeat Steps 1–5.

5. On your own, enter underlines into rows 7, 12, and 17. Then enter double underlines into rows 9 and 19. Remember to first position the cursor in the cell in which you want the dashes or double lines to begin and to then type a backslash followed by a dash (for dashed underlines) or an equal sign (for double underlines). Then copy the underline or double underline across the row using the procedure for copying text. The spreadsheet should look like Figure 3.3.

Figure 3.3

Underlines have been copied into the NET-INC spreadsheet.

```
A19: [W14] \=                                                        READY

          A         B         C         D         E        F        G
1  CALCULATING NET INCOME
2
3  INCOME        QTR1      QTR2      QTR3      QTR4     TOTAL   PERCENT
4  --------------------------------------------------------------------
5  SALARY        5200      5200      5500      5500
6  OTHER         1209       955       757      1320
7  --------------------------------------------------------------------
8  TOTAL
9  ====================================================================
10
11 EXPENSES
12 --------------------------------------------------------------------
13 RENT           925       925       925       925
14 UTILITIES      321       230       121       300
15 AUTO           300       366       519       521
16 OTHER          490       698       490       721
17 --------------------------------------------------------------------
18 TOTAL
19 ====================================================================
20 NET INCOME
01-Oct-92  04:25 PM            UNDO                              CAPS
```

Quick Reference

Copying

1. Position the cursor on the cell you want to copy.
2. Initiate Menu mode.
3. CHOOSE: Copy
4. Check to see that the cell(s) you're copying from are highlighted, and then press [Enter].
5. Position the cursor on the first cell in the range you're copying to.
6. To anchor the beginning of the range:
   TYPE: .
7. Highlight the cell(s) you're copying into, and then press [Enter].

COPYING FORMULAS

In this section you will enter formulas and then copy them into the appropriate cells. Here is an overview:

- In cell B8, you will type a formula that adds the amounts in cells B5 and B6 (B5+B6). You will then copy this formula into the range of cells B8..G8.

- In cell B18, you will type a formula that adds the amounts in the range B13..B16 [@SUM(B13..B16)]. You will then copy this formula into the range of cells B18..G18.

- In cell B20, you will type a formula that subtracts the expense total (B18) from the income total (B8) (B8-B18). You will then copy this formula into the range of cells B20..F20.

- In cell F5, you will type a formula that adds the quarterly salary amounts [@SUM(B5..E5)]. You will then copy this formula into cell F6.

- In cell F13, you will type a formula that adds the quarterly rent amounts [@SUM(B13..E13)]. You will then copy this formula into the range F13..F16.

- In cell G5, you will type a formula that requires an absolute reference to cell F8. The formula divides (/) the salary total (F5) by the total of all income totals (F8). Because you don't want the reference to cell F8 to change when you copy the formula, you make the reference to it absolute by preceding the column and row references with dollar signs ($). You will copy this formula into cell G6.

- In cell G13, you will type another formula that requires an absolute reference to cell F18 ($F$18). The formula divides (/) the rent total (F13) by the total of all expenses (F18) (+F13/$F$18). Again, because you don't want the reference to cell F18 to change when you copy the formula, you need to make the reference to it absolute by preceding the column and row references with dollar signs ($). You will copy this formula into cells G13..G16.

We will now proceed with entering and copying formulas. First, enter the formula +B5+B6 into cell B8, and then copy it into the range B8..G8:

1. Position the cursor in cell B8.

2. TYPE: +B5+B6
   PRESS: [Enter]

3. TYPE: /
    CHOOSE: Copy

4. Lotus is now prompting you to enter the cell range you are copying from. Lotus assumes you are copying from the cell the cursor is positioned on. Since this is a correct assumption:
    PRESS: Enter

5. Lotus is now waiting for you to specify the range of cells you are copying to. Since you are copying into more than one cell, you must anchor in place the reference to cell B8.
    TYPE: .
    PRESS: → *until the range B8..G8 is highlighted*
    PRESS: Enter

Position the cursor on each of the copied formulas while looking in the upper-left corner of the screen. Note that each formula has adjusted relative to its new position in the spreadsheet. With the cursor positioned on cell E8, the screen should look like Figure 3.4.

Figure 3.4

The formula to calculate Quarter 1's income total has been copied into the range B8..G8.

```
E8:  +E5+E6                                                              READY

              A              B        C        D        E        F        G
 1 CALCULATING NET INCOME
 2
 3  INCOME              QTR1     QTR2     QTR3     QTR4    TOTAL   PERCENT
 4  ----------------------------------------------------------------------
 5  SALARY              5200     5200     5500     5500
 6  OTHER               1209      955      757     1320
 7  ----------------------------------------------------------------------
 8  TOTAL               6409     6155     6257     6820        0         0
 9  ======================================================================
10
11 EXPENSES
12 ----------------------------------------------------------------------
13  RENT                 925      925      925      925
14  UTILITIES            321      230      121      300
15  AUTO                 300      366      519      521
16  OTHER                490      698      490      721
17 ----------------------------------------------------------------------
18  TOTAL
19  ======================================================================
20 NET INCOME
01-Oct-92  04:31 PM          UNDO                              CAPS
```

Perform the following steps to enter the rest of the formulas into the spreadsheet and to copy them into the appropriate cells:

1. Position the cursor in cell B18.
    TYPE: @SUM(B13..B16)
    PRESS: Enter

2. Copy this formula into the five cells to the right.

3. Position the cursor in cell B20.
   TYPE: +B8-B18
   PRESS: (Enter)

4. Copy this formula into the range B20..F20. Position the cursor on each of the copied formulas while looking in the upper-left corner of the screen. Note that each formula has adjusted relative to its new position in the spreadsheet (Figure 3.5).

Figure 3.5

Additional formulas have been copied into the spreadsheet.

```
E20: +E8-E18                                                              READY

         A          B         C         D         E        F       G
1  CALCULATING NET INCOME
2
3  INCOME         QTR1      QTR2      QTR3      QTR4     TOTAL   PERCENT
4  ----------------------------------------------------------------------
5  SALARY         5200      5200      5500      5500
6  OTHER          1209       955       757      1320
7  ----------------------------------------------------------------------
8  TOTAL          6409      6155      6257      6820       0       0
9  ======================================================================
10
11 EXPENSES
12 ----------------------------------------------------------------------
13 RENT            925       925       925       925
14 UTILITIES       321       230       121       300
15 AUTO            300       366       519       521
16 OTHER           490       698       490       721
17 ----------------------------------------------------------------------
18 TOTAL          2036      2219      2055      2467       0       0
19 ======================================================================
20 NET INCOME     4373      3936      4202      4353       0
01-Oct-92  04:32 PM          UNDO                                    CAPS
```

---

5. Position the cursor in cell F5.
   TYPE: @SUM(B5..E5)
   PRESS: (Enter)

6. Copy this formula into cell F6.

7. Position the cursor in cell F13.
   TYPE: @SUM(B13..E13)
   PRESS: (Enter)

8. Copy this formula into the three cells below.

9. Position the cursor in cell G5.
   TYPE: +F5/$F$8
   PRESS: (Enter)
   The number .834600 should be displaying in the cell. You will use the RANGE FORMAT command to format this column in the percent format later in this session.

10. Copy this formula into cell G6 (0.165399 is displaying in cell G6).

The screen should look like Figure 3.6. Position the cursor on the copied formula in cells F5 and F6; move the cursor back and forth. Note that the reference to cell F8 didn't adjust because the reference to cell F8 (in the formula) is absolute (designated by dollar signs).

Figure 3.6

A formula that includes an absolute reference has been entered into cell G5 and then copied into the cell below.

```
G6:  +F6/$F$8                                                            READY

           A           B           C           D           E           F         G
 1   CALCULATING NET INCOME
 2
 3   INCOME          QTR1        QTR2        QTR3        QTR4      TOTAL   PERCENT
 4   ------------------------------------------------------------------------------
 5   SALARY          5200        5200        5500        5500      21400  0.834600
 6   OTHER           1209         955         757        1320       4241  0.165399
 7   ------------------------------------------------------------------------------
 8   TOTAL           6409        6155        6257        6820      25641         1
 9   ==============================================================================
10
11   EXPENSES
12   ------------------------------------------------------------------------------
13   RENT             925         925         925         925       3700
14   UTILITIES        321         230         121         300        972
15   AUTO             300         366         519         521       1706
16   OTHER            490         698         490         721       2399
17   ------------------------------------------------------------------------------
18   TOTAL           2036        2219        2055        2467       8777         0
19   ==============================================================================
20   NET INCOME      4373        3936        4202        4353      16864
01-Oct-92  04:35 PM              UNDO                                       CAPS
```

---

11. Position the cursor in cell G13.

TYPE: +F13/$F$18

PRESS: (Enter)

12. Copy this formula into the three cells below.

Position the cursor on each of the copied formulas while looking in the upper-left corner of the screen. Note that each formula contains a reference to cell F18 because of the absolute reference to F18 in the formula. The screen should look like Figure 3.7.

MOVING

Moving text, data, and formulas uses the same procedure as does copying. The only difference in outcome is that the cell(s) you move items from are blank after you use the MOVE command. In this section you will use the MOVE command to move the text CALCULATING NET INCOME from cell A1 into cell B1 in the NET-INC spreadsheet. Then you will move the text back again.

Figure 3.7

A formula that includes an absolute reference has been entered into cell G13 and then copied to the three cells below.

```
G16:  +F16/$F$18                                                    READY

        A           B        C         D         E        F        G
1   CALCULATING NET INCOME
2
3   INCOME          QTR1     QTR2      QTR3      QTR4    TOTAL  PERCENT
4   ─────────────────────────────────────────────────────────────────
5   SALARY          5200     5200      5500      5500    21400 0.834600
6   OTHER           1209      955       757      1320     4241 0.165399
7   ─────────────────────────────────────────────────────────────────
8   TOTAL           6409     6155      6257      6820    25641        1
9   ═════════════════════════════════════════════════════════════════
10
11  EXPENSES
12  ─────────────────────────────────────────────────────────────────
13  RENT             925      925       925       925     3700 0.421556
14  UTILITIES        321      230       121       300      972 0.110743
15  AUTO             300      366       519       521     1706 0.194371
16  OTHER            490      698       490       721     2399 0.273328
17  ─────────────────────────────────────────────────────────────────
18  TOTAL           2036     2219      2055      2467     8777        1
19  ═════════════════════════════════════════════════════════════════
20  NET INCOME      4373     3936      4202      4353    16864
01-Oct-92  04:35 PM              UNDO                            CAPS
```

Perform the following steps:

1. The NET-INC spreadsheet should be displaying on the screen. To position the cursor on cell A1, the beginning of the range you're moving from:
   PRESS: (Home)

2. To initiate the MOVE command:
   PRESS: /
   CHOOSE: Move

3. Since the cursor is already highlighting the range you're moving from:
   PRESS: (Enter)

4. Now you need to position the cursor where the text should be moved to. Position the cursor in cell B1, and then press (Enter).

   The text CALCULATING NET INCOME should be positioned in cell B1.

5. To move the text CALCULATING NET INCOME back to cell A1, position the cursor on cell B1 (the cell that contains the text you're moving).

6. To initiate the MOVE command:
   PRESS: /
   CHOOSE: Move

7. Since the cursor is already highlighting the range you're moving from:
   PRESS: (Enter)

8. Now you need to position the cursor where the text should be moved to. Position the cursor in cell A1, and then press [Enter].

The text CALCULATING NET INCOME should again be positioned in cell A1.

....

Quick Reference   1. Position the cursor on the first cell in the range you want to move.
                        2. Initiate Menu mode.
Moving   3. CHOOSE: Move
                        4. Highlight the cell(s) you're moving, and then press [Enter].
                        5. Position the cursor where you want the moved text, numbers, or formulas to be positioned, and then press [Enter].

....

FORMATTING COMMANDS

In this section you will use a number of formatting commands to improve the appearance of this spreadsheet and to make it easier to read. Formatting commands make the numbers in a spreadsheet more self-evident in meaning. For example, if a dollar amount is displayed as $42,554.50, its meaning is more self-evident than if it were displayed as 42554.5. Table 3.1 describes the different ways you can format numbers. **Global formatting commands** affect every cell in a spreadsheet. **Range formatting commands** affect only the range of cells you specify. *Range commands take precedence over global commands. Therefore, if you format a range of cells in the percent format and then globally format the entire spreadsheet in the currency format, the range of cells displaying percents won't change to the currency format.*

Table 3.1	Option	Purpose
Formatting Options	Fixed	Displays a minus sign for negative numbers, and up to 15 decimal places. For decimal values, the Fixed format will display a leading zero.
	Sci(entific)	Displaces numbers in scientific (exponential) notation, with up to 15 decimal places in the mantissa and an exponent from -99 to +99.

Table 3.1 Formatting Options (concluded)	Currency	Displays numbers with a leading dollar sign and thousands separated by a comma. In addition, you can specify up to 15 decimal places. Negative numbers are displayed with either a leading minus sign or parentheses (depending on the Worksheet Global Default Other International setting for negatives).
	(Comma)	Displays numbers with thousands separated by a comma. In addition, you can specify up to 15 decimal places. The Comma format is the same as the Currency format without a dollar sign. Negative numbers are displayed with either a leading minus sign or parentheses (depending on the Worksheet Global Default Other International setting for negatives).
	General	Displays numbers without a comma and no trailing zeros to the right of the decimal point. Negative numbers are displayed with a leading minus sign.
	+/-	Displays a bar of minus (-) signs, plus (+) signs, or a period (.) that equal the number in the entry. Plus signs indicate a positive value; minus signs indicate a negative value. A period indicates the value is between -1 and 1.
	Percent	Displays numbers as percentages (that is, multiplied by 100), with up to 15 decimal places and a trailing percent sign.
	Date	Displays a Julian date (a number between 1 and 73050) as a date in the format you select. The number 1 represents January 1, 1900; the number 73050 represents December 31, 2099.
	Text	Displays formulas as they appear when you type them in rather than their computed values. After formatting, the cell still contains a value (not a label).
	Hidden	Displays data in a range as invisible; the data still exists in the range, however.
	Reset	Resets a range to the global cell format, as specified by the WORKSHEET GLOBAL FORMAT command.

In this section, we lead you through formatting the NET-INC spreadsheet so that it looks like Figure 3.2. You will perform the following tasks:

1. Globally format the spreadsheet in the currency format (WORKSHEET GLOBAL FORMAT CURRENCY).

2. Globally widen the columns to 12 characters (WORKSHEET GLOBAL COLUMN-WIDTH).

3. Range format column G in the percent format (RANGE FORMAT PERCENT).

4. Experiment with realigning the column headings.

GLOBAL COMMANDS: FORMATTING NUMBERS AND WIDENING COLUMNS

The NET-INC spreadsheet should still be displaying on the screen. In this section you will practice using global commands by first globally formatting this spreadsheet in the currency format to zero (0) decimal places. You will then globally format the spreadsheet in the currency format to two decimals, which will cause asterisks to display in certain cells (those not wide enough to accommodate all the numbers). To get rid of the asterisks you will use a global command to widen all the columns in the spreadsheet. *For global commands, it doesn't matter where the cursor is positioned because every cell in the spreadsheet is affected. However, when you are using range commands, position the cursor at the beginning of the range to be formatted.*

Perform the following steps to globally format the NET-INC spreadsheet in the currency format to zero (0) decimal places:

1. To initiate a global command:
   TYPE: /
   CHOOSE: Worksheet, Global
   With the cursor in cell A1, the screen should look like Figure 3.8.

2. CHOOSE: Format, Currency

3. To specify zero (0) decimals:
   TYPE: 0
   PRESS: (Enter)
   The screen should look like Figure 3.9. Note that the numbers in the percent column—which are mostly zeros because the cells were formatted to zero decimal places—are displaying with a leading dollar sign. Shortly, you will use a range command to format the range G5..G18 in the percent format.

Figure 3.8

The Global menu option has been chosen, and the Global settings sheet is displaying.

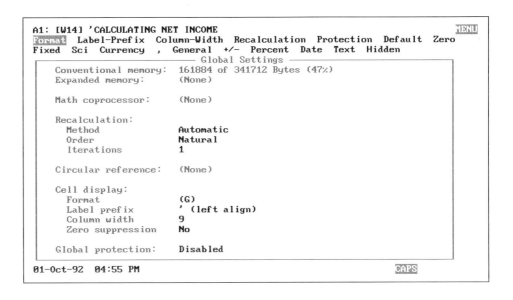

```
A1: [W14] 'CALCULATING NET INCOME                          MENU
Format Label-Prefix Column-Width Recalculation Protection Default Zero
Fixed  Sci  Currency  ,  General  +/-  Percent  Date  Text  Hidden
──────────────────── Global Settings ────────────────────
    Conventional memory:  161884 of 341712 Bytes (47%)
    Expanded memory:      (None)

    Math coprocessor:     (None)

    Recalculation:
      Method              Automatic
      Order               Natural
      Iterations          1

    Circular reference:   (None)

    Cell display:
      Format              (G)
      Label prefix        ' (left align)
      Column width        9
      Zero suppression    No

    Global protection:    Disabled

01-Oct-92  04:55 PM                                         CAPS
```

Figure 3.9

The spreadsheet has been globally formatted in the currency format to 0 decimal places.

```
A1: [W14] 'CALCULATING NET INCOME                         READY

         A          B        C        D        E        F        G
 1 CALCULATING NET INCOME
 2
 3 INCOME          QTR1     QTR2     QTR3     QTR4     TOTAL   PERCENT
 4 ──────────────────────────────────────────────────────────────
 5 SALARY         $5,200   $5,200   $5,500   $5,500  $21,400      $1
 6 OTHER          $1,209     $955     $757   $1,320   $4,241      $0
 7 ──────────────────────────────────────────────────────────────
 8 TOTAL          $6,409   $6,155   $6,257   $6,820  $25,641      $1
 9 ══════════════════════════════════════════════════════════════
10
11 EXPENSES
12 ──────────────────────────────────────────────────────────────
13 RENT             $925     $925     $925     $925   $3,700      $0
14 UTILITIES        $321     $230     $121     $300     $972      $0
15 AUTO             $300     $366     $519     $521   $1,706      $0
16 OTHER            $490     $698     $490     $721   $2,399      $0
17 ──────────────────────────────────────────────────────────────
18 TOTAL          $2,036   $2,219   $2,055   $2,467   $8,777      $1
19 ══════════════════════════════════════════════════════════════
20 NET INCOME     $4,373   $3,936   $4,202   $4,353  $16,864
01-Oct-92  04:56 PM              UNDO                       CAPS
```

Perform the following to see what happens when the NET-INC spreadsheet is globally formatted in the currency format to two decimal places:

1. To initiate the GLOBAL FORMAT command:
   TYPE: /
   CHOOSE: <u>W</u>orksheet, <u>G</u>lobal, <u>F</u>ormat, <u>C</u>urrency

2. To specify two decimals:
    PRESS: [Enter]
    The screen should look like Figure 3.10. Lotus displays asterisks where the
    columns aren't wide enough to display the numbers in the cells.

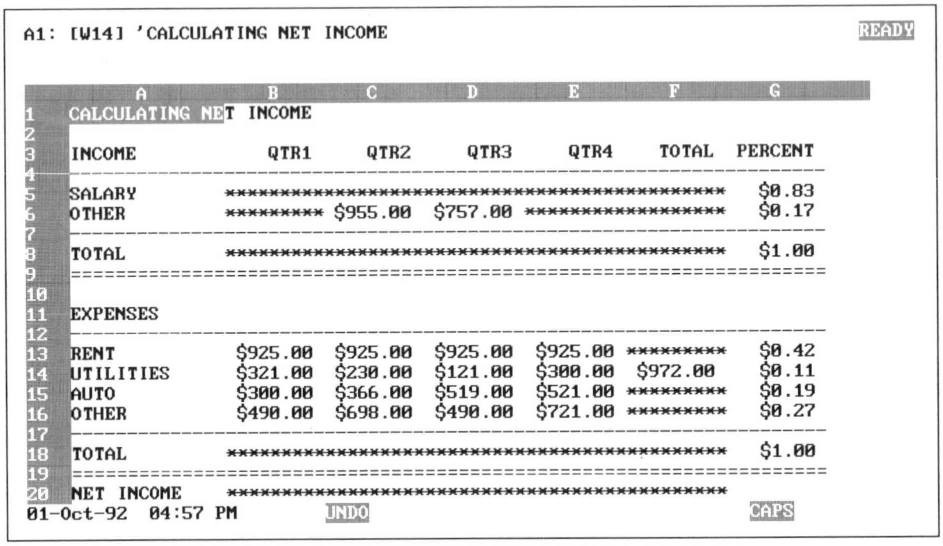

Figure 3.10

Because the
spreadsheet was
globally formatted
in the currency
format to 2 decimal
places, asterisks
are diplaying since
the columns aren't
wide enough to
display the for-
matted numbers.

```
A1: [W14] 'CALCULATING NET INCOME                                              READY

         A         B         C         D         E         F         G
 1  CALCULATING NET INCOME
 2
 3  INCOME         QTR1      QTR2      QTR3      QTR4     TOTAL   PERCENT
 4
 5  SALARY      ***************************************************   $0.83
 6  OTHER       ********* $955.00 $757.00 *******************   $0.17
 7
 8  TOTAL       ***************************************************   $1.00
 9  ============================================================
10
11  EXPENSES
12
13  RENT        $925.00   $925.00   $925.00   $925.00 *********   $0.42
14  UTILITIES   $321.00   $230.00   $121.00   $300.00  $972.00   $0.11
15  AUTO        $300.00   $366.00   $519.00   $521.00 *********   $0.19
16  OTHER       $490.00   $698.00   $490.00   $721.00 *********   $0.27
17
18  TOTAL       ***************************************************   $1.00
19  ============================================================
20  NET INCOME  ***************************************************
01-Oct-92  04:57 PM              UNDO                                    CAPS
```

---

1. Initiate Menu mode.
2. CHOOSE: Worksheet, Global, Format
3. Choose a formatting option and then specify the number of decimal
    places.

To globally widen the spreadsheet columns to 12 characters each:

1. Initiate a global command:
    TYPE: /
    CHOOSE: Worksheet, Global, Column-Width

2. Specify 12 characters:
    TYPE: 12
    PRESS: [Enter]
    All the numbers should be displaying in the spreadsheet. Because of the
    widened columns, the entire spreadsheet can no longer be seen on the screen at
    once.

Quick Reference

Widening Every Column

1. Initiate Menu mode.
2. CHOOSE: <u>W</u>orksheet, <u>G</u>lobal, <u>C</u>olumn-width
3. Type a number that corresponds to the new column width and press ⌈Enter⌋. The number you type should be at least as large as the widest entry in the column.

RANGE COMMANDS: FORMATTING NUMBERS AND REALIGNING LABELS

In this section you will use a range command to format the percent column (G) in the percent format. In addition, you will practice using a range command to realign labels. *Remember, before using a range command, position the cursor at the beginning of the range you want to format.*

To format the percent column (G5..G18) in the percent format:

1. Position the cursor in cell G5.

2. TYPE: /
   CHOOSE: <u>R</u>ange, <u>F</u>ormat, <u>P</u>ercent

3. To accept two decimals:
   PRESS: ⌈Enter⌋

4. To specify the range of cells you want to format:
   PRESS: ⌈↓⌋ *until the range G5..G18 is highlighted*
   PRESS: ⌈Enter⌋
   Column G should now be displayed in the percent format.

(Note: Formatting is <u>not</u> the same as copying. You don't have to anchor cell G5 before highlighting all the cells through G18.)

Quick Reference

Formatting a Range

1. Position the cursor in the beginning of the range to be formatted.
2. TYPE: /
   CHOOSE: <u>R</u>ange, <u>F</u>ormat
3. Choose a formatting option, and then specify the number of decimal places that each cell should be formatted to.
4. Highlight the range of cells you want to format, and then press ⌈Enter⌋.

To practice realigning labels in a range of cells, you will center and then right-align the headings in the range B3..G3. Finally, you will save the NET-INC spreadsheet.

1. Position the cursor in cell B3.

2. TYPE: /
    CHOOSE: <u>R</u>ange, <u>L</u>abel, <u>C</u>enter

3. To specify the range of cells B3..G3:
    PRESS: ⟶ *until the range B3..G3 is highlighted*
    PRESS: ⟨Enter⟩
    The headings should now appear centered in the cells.

4. On your own, realign the headings so they are again right-aligned in the cells.

5. Save NET-INC onto the Advantage Diskette.

Quick Reference

Realigning a Range of Labels

1. Initiate Menu mode.
2. CHOOSE: <u>R</u>ange, <u>L</u>abel
3. Choose Left, Right, or Center.
4. Highlight the range of headings that you want to realign, and then press ⟨Enter⟩.

@AVG

The **@AVG function** makes it easy to find the average value of a range of cells. Using the @AVG function involves specifying the range of cells to be averaged. In this section you will insert some text in the range A23..A26 (Figure 3.11) and then use the @AVG function in cell B24 to determine the average quarterly net income amount. When entering functions, don't include any spaces in the function (unless you're including text in an @IF function, which is a procedure described in this session).

Figure 3.11

The NET-INC spreadsheet after a statistics section has been added. This section uses the @AVG, @MIN, and @MAX functions.

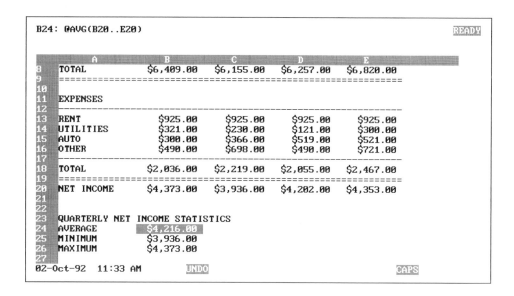

```
B24: @AVG(B20..E20)                                              READY

            A           B           C           D           E
 8   TOTAL           $6,409.00   $6,155.00   $6,257.00   $6,820.00
 9   =================================================================
10
11   EXPENSES
12   -----------------------------------------------------------------
13   RENT              $925.00     $925.00     $925.00     $925.00
14   UTILITIES         $321.00     $230.00     $121.00     $300.00
15   AUTO              $300.00     $366.00     $519.00     $521.00
16   OTHER             $490.00     $698.00     $490.00     $721.00
17   -----------------------------------------------------------------
18   TOTAL           $2,036.00   $2,219.00   $2,055.00   $2,467.00
19   =================================================================
20   NET INCOME      $4,373.00   $3,936.00   $4,202.00   $4,353.00
21
22
23   QUARTERLY NET INCOME STATISTICS
24   AVERAGE          $4,216.00
25   MINIMUM          $3,936.00
26   MAXIMUM          $4,373.00
27
02-Oct-92   11:33 AM          UNDO                            CAPS
```

1. Position the cursor in the following cells and type in the corresponding text:

Move to Cell	TYPE:
A23	QUARTERLY NET INCOME STATISTICS
A24	AVERAGE
A25	MINIMUM
A26	MAXIMUM

2. Position the cursor in cell B24 so that you can type the @AVG function.

3. Since you are determining the average value in the range of cells B20..E20:
   TYPE: @AVG(B20..E20)
   PRESS: (Enter)
   The number $4,216.00 should now be displaying in cell B24. *Note that the number is displaying in the currency format—in this session you globally formatted the spreadsheet in the currency format to two decimal places. Any number you type—into any cell—will now appear in the currency format unless you use the RANGE FORMAT command to format a range of cells.*

Quick Reference

@AVG(Range)

To determine the average of the values stored in a range of cells, position the cursor in the cell in which the average should appear. Then type @AVG followed by an open parenthesis, the range of cells that contains the values to be averaged, and then a closing parenthesis. Press (Enter) to put the formula in the cell. Don't include any spaces in the formula.

@MIN

The **@MIN function** makes it easy to find the minimum value in a range of cells. In this step you will determine the minimum quarterly net income amount using the following: @MIN(B20..E20)

Perform the following steps:

1. Position the cursor in cell B25.

2. TYPE: @MIN(B20..E20)
    PRESS: [Enter]
    The number $3,936.00 should now be displaying in cell B25.

Quick Reference

@MIN(Range)

To determine the minimum of the values stored in a range of cells, position the cursor in the cell in which the minimum should appear, and type @MIN followed by an open parenthesis, the range of cells that contains the values, and then a closing parenthesis. Press [Enter] to put the formula in the cell. Don't include any spaces in the formula.

@MAX

The **@MAX function** makes it easy to find the maximum value in a range of cells. In this step you will determine the maximum quarterly net income amount using the following function: @MAX(B20..E20)

Perform the following steps:

1. Position the cursor in cell B26.

2. TYPE: @MAX(B20..E20)
    PRESS: [Enter]
    The number $4,373.00 should now be displaying in cell B26.

3. Save the NET-INC spreadsheet onto the Advantage Diskette. (If you have forgotten how to save a spreadsheet, refer to Session 2.)

....

Quick Reference

@MAX(Range)

To determine the maximum of the values stored in a range of cells, position the cursor in the cell in which the maximum should appear, and type @MAX followed by an open parenthesis, the range of cells that contains the values, and then a closing parenthesis. Press (Enter) to put the formula in the cell. Don't include any spaces in the formula.

....

@DATE

In this section you will retrieve the file called BILLS from the Advantage Diskette so you can practice using the @IF and @DATE functions. Figure 3.12 shows the completed BILLS spreadsheet. The objective of this spreadsheet is to keep track of your bills by calculating the number of days until the bill is due and the status of the bill (OVERDUE or O.K.). The numbers in the Days to Go column are calculated by subtracting the Current Date from the Due Date. The @IF function, described in the next section, determines what text displays in the Bill Status column.

Figure 3.12

The completed BILLS spreadsheet

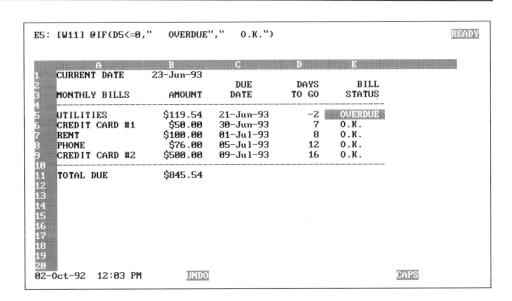

The **@DATE function** enables you to store a date in a cell as a number so that you can perform calculations on the date. You will use the @DATE function to store the current date in cell B1 and also to store due dates in the range of cells C5..C9. (So that you can see if your answers are correct, you will use the current date that is displaying in Figure 3.12—that is, June 23, 1993.) In the BILLS spreadsheet, once the dates have been entered using the @DATE function, you can determine how many days are left before a bill is due by subtracting the Current Date from the Due Date.

The format of the @DATE function is @DATE(YY,MM,DD). Once a date has been entered using the @DATE function, a number, such as 34143, will appear in the cell. This is the number of days that have passed since January 1, 1900. By itself, this number isn't meaningful; you need to format it to be displayed in Lotus 1-2-3's date format.

Perform the following steps to retrieve the BILLS spreadsheet, enter the current date in cell B1, and then use a range command to format cell B1 in the date format:

1. Retrieve the BILLS spreadsheet from the Advantage Diskette.

2. Position the cursor in cell B1 so that you can type in the current date.

3. TYPE: @DATE(93,6,23)
    PRESS: (Enter)
    The screen should look like Figure 3.13.

Figure 3.13

The current date has been entered using the @DATE function. The number of days that have passed since January 1, 1900, is displaying in cell B1.

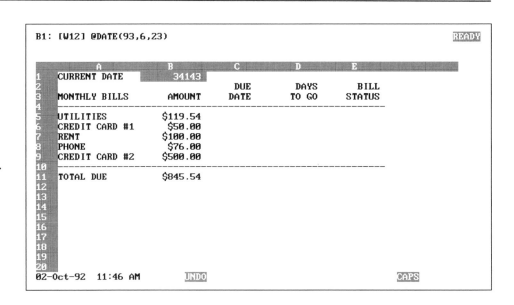

The number 34143 stands for the number of days that have passed since January 1, 1900. In the next few steps you will add the date format to this cell.

4. Make sure the cursor is positioned in cell B1.

5. To initiate the FORMAT command so that you can format cell B1 in the date format:
TYPE: /
CHOOSE: Range, Format, Date

6. Lotus 1-2-3 is now prompting you to choose a way to display the date. To format the date using the standard long form (DD-MMM-YY):
CHOOSE: 1

7. Lotus now wants you to specify the range of cells to format. Since the cursor is highlighting the cell you want to format:
PRESS: Enter
The screen should now look like Figure 3.14.

Figure 3.14

Cell B1 has been formatted using the date format.

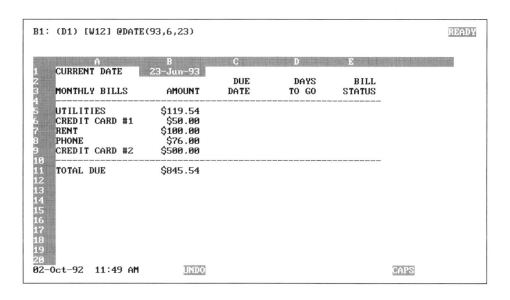

In the next few steps you will enter dates into the range C5..C9 and then format the range C5..C9 in the date format. (Remember, if you type something in incorrectly, use F2 (Edit) to correct the entry or position the cursor on the cell and retype the contents.)

1. Position the cursor in cell C5 and type in the following:
TYPE: @DATE(93,6,21)
PRESS: Enter
The number 34141 should be displaying in the cell.

2. Position the cursor in cell C6 and type in the following:
TYPE: @DATE(93,6,30)
PRESS: Enter
The number 34150 should be displaying in the cell.

3. Position the cursor is cell C7 and type in the following:
   TYPE: @DATE(93,7,1)
   PRESS: (Enter)
   The number 34151 should be displaying in the cell.

4. Position the cursor in cell C8 and type in the following:
   TYPE: @DATE(93,7,5)
   PRESS: (Enter)
   The number 34155 should be displaying in the cell.

5. Position the cursor in cell C9 and type in the following:
   TYPE: @DATE(93,7,9)
   PRESS: (Enter)
   The number 34159 should be displaying in the cell. The screen should look
   like Figure 3.15. In the next few steps you will format the range C5..C9 in the
   date format.

Figure 3.15

Dates have been
entered into the
Due Date column.
The dates haven't
yet been formatted.

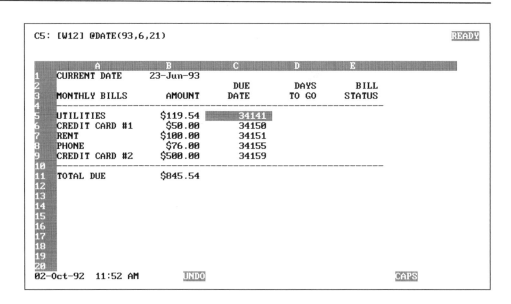

6. Position the cursor in cell C5 and then issue the following commands to
   initiate the FORMAT DATE command:
   TYPE: /
   CHOOSE: Range, Format, Date

7. To format the date using the standard long form:
   CHOOSE: 1

8. Lotus is now waiting for you to type in the range of cells you want to format:
    PRESS: ⬇ *four times to highlight the range C5..C9*
    PRESS: (Enter)
    The screen should now look like Figure 3.16.

Figure 3.16

The dates in the Due Date column have been formatted using the date format.

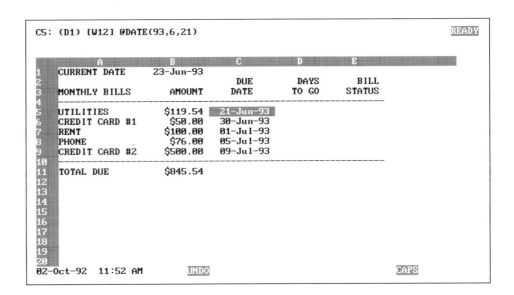

Quick Reference

@DATE(YY,MM,DD)

1. Type @DATE followed by an open parenthesis, the numbers that correspond to the year, month, and day (separated by commas), and then a closing parenthesis. Press (Enter).
2. Format the cell(s) that contain the @DATE function(s) using the date format.

CALCULATING WITH DATES

In the next few steps you will type a formula into cell D5 that will calculate the number of days until a bill must be paid. You will then copy the formula into the four cells below D5. This formula subtracts the Current Date (B1) from the Due Date to determine how many days are left before a bill is due. *Every formula in this column must refer to cell B1. Since you will copy the formula down the column, you will need to prepare this formula to be copied by including an absolute reference to cell B1. (Absolute referencing was described earlier in this session.)*

1. Position the cursor in cell D5, and type the following formula:
    TYPE: +C5-$B$1
    PRESS: Enter
    The answer -2 should be displaying in cell D5. This particular bill is two days
    overdue.

2. The cursor should be positioned on cell D5. To initiate the COPY command:
    TYPE: /
    CHOOSE: Copy

3. To tell Lotus you're copying from D5:
    PRESS: Enter

4. To tell Lotus you're copying into the range D5..D9, first anchor D5:
    PRESS: .
    PRESS: ⬇ *to highlight the range D5..D9*
    PRESS: Enter
    The screen should look like Figure 3.17.

Figure 3.17

The Days to Go
formula has been
entered and then
copied. The for-
mula includes an
absolute reference
to cell B1 because
every formula in
the column must
refer to cell B1.

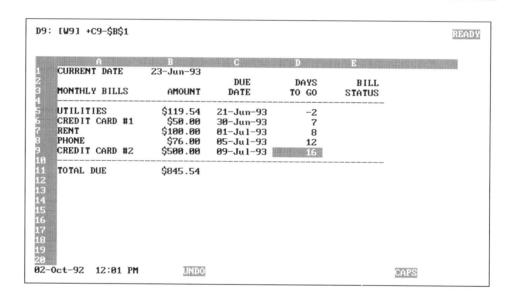

@IF

The **@IF function** enables you to tell Lotus to perform a test and to take one of
two actions depending on whether the outcome is "true" or "false." If the outcome
of the test is "false," a   different action is performed. The format for the @IF
function is @IF(TEST,TRUE,FALSE). The @IF function is used in the Bill

Status column. Cell E5 contains @IF(D5<=0,"OVERDUE","O.K."). This formula does the following:

- Tests to see if the amount in cell D5 is less than or equal to 0 (D5<=0).
- If the test is true, displays the text "OVERDUE" in cell E5.
- If the test is false, displays the text "O.K" in cell E5.

Perform the following steps to put this formula in the Bill Status column:

1. To enter a formula into cell E5, position the cursor in cell E5:
   TYPE: @IF(D5<=0,"OVERDUE","O.K")
   PRESS: (Enter)
   The screen should look like Figure 3.18.

Figure 3.18

A formula has been entered into cell E5 that uses the @IF function. If the amount in cell D5 is less than or equal to zero, the text "OVERDUE" will display in cell E5; otherwise the text "O.K" will display in cell E5.

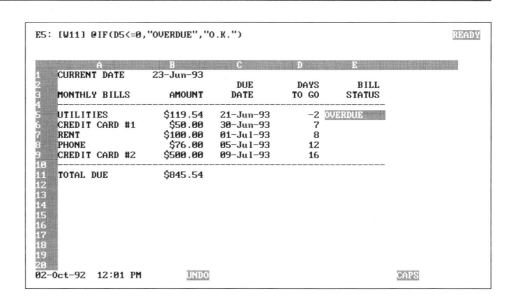

Note that the text "OVERDUE" appears very close to the amount in the column to the left. A way to fix this is to edit the formula in cell E5 (using (F2)) and insert a few spaces before the text within the quotes. Do the following to edit the formula:

2. The cursor should be positioned on cell E5. To edit the cell:
   PRESS: (F2)
   PRESS: (←) *until the cursor is beneath the "O" of "OVERDUE"*
   PRESS: Space Bar *three times*
   PRESS: (→) *until the cursor is beneath the "O" of "O.K."*
   PRESS: Space Bar *three times*
   PRESS: (Enter)
   The text should now appear farther away from the number to the left.

3. To copy the formula down the column, perform the following steps:
    TYPE: /
    CHOOSE: Copy
    PRESS: Enter
    TYPE: .
    PRESS: ↓ *four times to highlight the range E5..E9*
    PRESS: Enter
    The BILLS spreadsheet is now complete and should look like Figure 3.12.

4. Use Menu mode to save this spreadsheet file onto the Advantage Diskette as
    BILLS. (Saving was described in Session 2.)

CIRCULAR REFERENCES: AVOID THEM

In this section we will show you what circular references are, why they are bad,
and how to correct them. A **circular reference** occurs when a formula in a cell
directly or indirectly references the cell that it is in. Consider that whenever
anything (labels or values) is typed into a spreadsheet, the spreadsheet
recalculates. A formula that contains a circular reference will keep including in the
calculations the answer in the cell it is in.

One of the best ways to understand what circular references are is to create one. In
the steps below you will clear RAM and then create a circular reference. We will
then lead you through correcting the circular reference.

1. To clear RAM, you must use the Worksheet group of commands:
    TYPE: /
    CHOOSE: Worksheet, Erase, Yes

2. Type the number 10 into cells A1, A2, and A3.

3. Position the cursor in cell A4.

4. To cause a circular reference:
    TYPE: @SUM(A1..A4)
    PRESS: Enter
    The screen should look like Figure 3.19. The correct answer is now displaying
    in cell A4; however, the message CIRC is also displaying on the bottom of the
    screen.

Figure 3.19

Circular reference. Even though the correct answer is displaying in cell A4, the CIRC indicator on the bottom of the screen indicates that the formula's logic is incorrect.

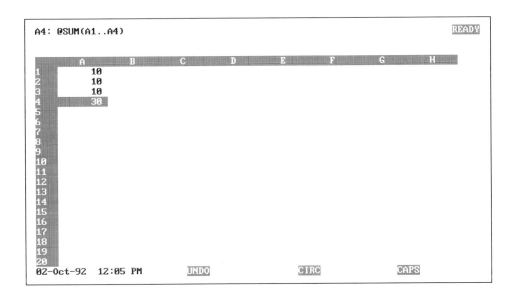

5. To cause the wrong answer to display in cell A4, position the cursor in any cell outside of the range A1..A4.
    TYPE: abc
    PRESS: (Enter)
    The screen should look similar to Figure 3.20. The answer "60" should be displaying because the spreadsheet recalculated and added A1..A4 (10+10+10+30). The number in cell A4 will get larger each time you type something into the spreadsheet. *You cannot have circular references in your spreadsheets because incorrect answers will be calculated.*

Figure 3.20

Automatic recalculation. Since the spreadsheet contains a circular reference, after you type "abc" (or anything) into it, the formula in cell A4 will recalculate and display the wrong answer.

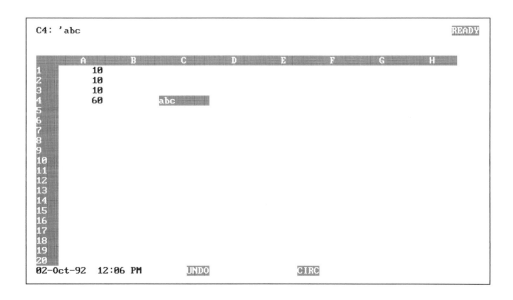

6. In this case, we know what cell contains the circular reference. But what if you are working with a large spreadsheet that contains hundreds of formulas and you see the CIRC message on the bottom of the screen? How would you know what formula contains the circular reference? To determine what cell contains the circular reference, use the **WORKSHEET STATUS** command as follows:
TYPE: /
CHOOSE: Worksheet, Status
The screen should look similar to Figure 3.21. The circular reference is shown to be in cell A4.

Figure 3.21

The WORKSHEET STATUS command. If a spreadsheet contains a circular reference, the cell containing the circular reference will be listed on this screen.

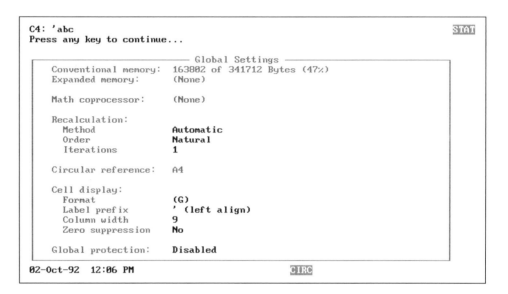

7. Now you know where the circular reference is. To return to the spreadsheet to correct it:
PRESS: Space Bar

8. To correct a circular reference, simply position the cursor on the cell that contains the processing error, and edit it using (F2), as follows:
Position the cursor on cell A4.
PRESS: (F2)
The contents of cell A4 should be displaying on the top of the screen.
PRESS: (←) *until the cursor is positioned beneath the number 4*
PRESS: (Delete) *once*
TYPE: 3
PRESS: (Enter)
The formula should now be correct, and the circular reference should have disappeared. The number 30 should now be displaying in cell A4.

Quick Reference

Locating Circular References

1. Initiate Menu mode.
2. CHOOSE: Worksheet, Status
   The STATUS command lists the reference to the cell that contains the circular reference.
3. To exit the STATUS command:
   PRESS: Space Bar
4. Edit the cell that contains the circular reference.

SUMMARY

The procedure of copying text, underlines, and formulas, is one you will use over and over when creating spreadsheets. Remember that when copying formulas, you may need to include an absolute reference (such as $A$3) rather than a relative reference (such as A3) in the formula before you copy it. The rule of thumb is that if a series of formulas refers to the same cell, you will need to include an absolute reference to that cell before you copy the formula.

The @AVG, @MIN, @MAX, @IF, and @DATE functions are commonly used in spreadsheets. Remember to include the @ before the function name and not to include any spaces when typing the formula (unless you're including text in an @IF formula).

Once you've entered formulas and numeric data into a spreadsheet, you will probably want to add currency, percent, fixed, or other formats. You can format cells with range or global commands; range commands take precedence over global commands.

When you see the CIRC message on the bottom of your screen, you know you have a circular reference in one or more of your formulas. Circular references cause your formulas to produce incorrect results. To determine which cell contains a circular reference, use the WORKSHEET STATUS command.

COMMAND SUMMARY

The table on the next page provides a list of the commands and procedures covered in this session.

Table 3.2

Command Summary

Copy the contents of a range of cells	Position the cursor on the first cell in the range you're copying from, /, Copy, highlight the cell(s) you're copying from, (Enter), highlight the cell(s) you're copying to, (Enter)
Move the contents of a range of cells	Position the cursor on the first cell in the range you're moving from, /, Move, highlight the cell(s) you're moving from, (Enter), highlight the cell(s) you're moving to, (Enter)
Globally format a spreadsheet	/, Worksheet, Global, Format, choose a formatting option, (Enter), highlight the range of cells to be formatted, (Enter)
Format a range of numbers	Position the cursor at the beginning of the range to be formatted, /, Range, Format, choose a formatting option, (Enter), highlight the range of cells to be formatted, (Enter)
Realign a range of labels	Position the cursor at the beginning of the range to be formatted, /, Range, Label, choose Left, Right, or Center, highlight the range of headings to realign, (Enter)
Locate a circular reference	/, Worksheet, Status, after determining which cell contains the circular reference, press Space Bar to display the spreadsheet, press (F2) to edit the cell with the circular reference.

KEY TERMS

absolute cell reference   Cell reference in an electronic spreadsheet formula that doesn't adjust when it is copied. Compare **relative cell reference**.

@AVG function   Lotus 1-2-3 function used to determine the average amount of values stored in a range of spreadsheet cells.

BACKSLASH-FILL   Lotus 1-2-3 command that enables you fill a cell with whatever character you type in after a backslash (\ ).

circular reference   In Lotus 1-2-3, the situation created when a formula includes a cell reference to the cell the formula is in.

COPY   Lotus 1-2-3 command that enables you to copy the contents of one or more cells into another area of the spreadsheet.

@DATE function   Lotus 1-2-3 function that enables the user to store a date in a cell as a number so that calculations can be performed using the date.

global formatting command   Lotus 1-2-3 command that affects every cell in the spreadsheet, as opposed to a range of cells.

@IF function   Lotus 1-2-3 function that enables the user to perform a test; if the outcome of the test is "true," one action is performed. If the outcome of the test is "false," a different action is performed.

@MAX function   A Lotus 1-2-3 function that is used to determine the maximum amount of values stored in a range of spreadsheet cells.

@MIN function   Lotus 1-2-3 function used to determine the minimum amount of values stored in a range of spreadsheet cells.

MOVE   Lotus 1-2-3 command that enables you to move the contents of one or more cells into another area of the spreadsheet. Unlike when using the **COPY** command, the cells you moved from are empty after you use this command.

range formatting command   Formatting commands that affect a range of cells in a spreadsheet. Compare **global formatting commands**.

relative cell reference   Cell reference in an electronic spreadsheet formula that adjusts when it is copied. Compare **absolute cell reference**.

WORKSHEET STATUS   Lotus 1-2-3 command that enables you to determine what cell contains a circular message.

EXERCISES

SHORT ANSWER

1. Cell A5 was formatted in the currency format using a range command. Then with a global command, the spreadsheet was formatted in the percent format. How is cell A5 formatted?
2. What is the difference between an absolute cell address and a relative cell address? Why is it relevant to understand the difference?
3. Describe the procedure for creating an underline.
4. If you want to copy data into more than one cell, what key must you press to anchor the first cell in the range you're copying to?
5. What is a circular reference? Why don't you want to see CIRC in the bottom-center of the screen? What command would you use to determine what cell contains a circular reference?
6. Cell A1 contains the number 10. Cell A2 contains 25. Cell A3 contains 32. What would you put in cell A6 to determine the average of A1, A2, and A3?
7. If you want a date to be stored as a value with which you can do calculations, what would you type to store March 21, 1992, in a cell?
8. Cell A1 contains the number 25. Cell A2 contains 32. Describe what a formula in cell B1 would look like that does the following: If the number in cell A2 is greater than the number in cell A1, add the two numbers; otherwise put a zero in cell B1.

9. Cell B5 contains the current date @DATE(93,5,16). Cell B6 contains the invoice date @DATE(93,3,9). What formula would you put in cell B8 to determine the number of days that have passed?

10. What do all Lotus 1-2-3 functions have in common?

HANDS-ON

1. Create the spreadsheet pictured in Figure 3.22. Be sure to perform the following procedures:

Figure 3.22

The INCOME-1 spreadsheet

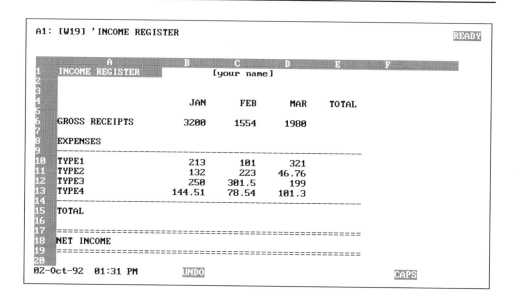

a. As displayed in Figure 3.22, type the text and numbers into the appropriate cells. (Be sure you type your name into cell C1.) Also, copy underlines into rows 9, 14, 17, and 19.

b. Type a formula into cell E6 that adds the three amounts to the left of it.

c. Type a formula into cell E10 that adds the three amounts to the left of it. Copy this formula into the three cells below E10.

d. Type a formula into cell B15 that adds the four expense amounts above it. Copy this formula into the three cells to the right of B15.

e. Type a formula into cell B18 that subtracts the total expense amount from the gross receipt amount. Copy this formula into the three cells to the right of B18.

f. Format all the cells that contain numbers in the currency format to two decimal places. If necessary, widen columns.

g. Save this spreadsheet onto the Advantage Diskette as INCOME-1.

h. Print INCOME-1 in both the as-displayed and cell-formulas formats.

2. To practice entering formulas, using absolute references, and copying, retrieve a copy of the QTR-DATA spreadsheet from the Advantage Diskette.
   a. Include a percentage column in column F. Make sure to do the following:
      - Include an absolute reference to cell E10 in the formula in cell F4.
      - Copy the formula in cell F4 into the four cells below it.
      - Format column F in the percent format.
   b. Include single underlines in rows 3 and 9, and a double underline in row 11.
   c. Position the cursor in the following cells and type in the corresponding text:

Move to Cell	TYPE:
A13	QUARTER 1: EXPENSE STATISTICS
A15	AVERAGE
A16	MINIMUM
A17	MAXIMUM

   d. Type functions into the range B15..B17 to calculate average, minimum, and maximum statistics (based on the range B10..D10).
   e. Type your name into cell B1.
   f. Save QTR-DATA onto the Advantage Diskette.
   g. Print QTR-DATA in both the as-displayed and cell-formulas formats.

3. Create a spreadsheet called WIDE on your Advantage Diskette. The first half of the spreadsheet is pictured in Figure 3.23(a) and the second half is pictured in Figure 3.23(b). This spreadsheet projects expenses out for 10 years, starting in 1991. You will type formulas into column C that will project 1991 expenses. Then you will copy these formulas through column L.

Figure 3.23 (a)

The first half of the WIDE spreadsheet

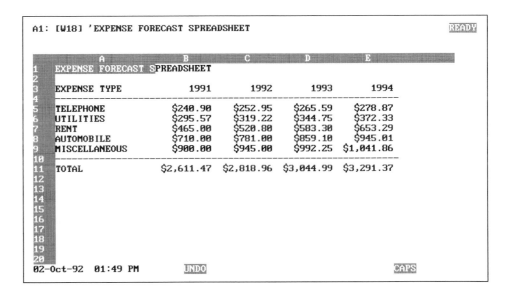

Figure 3.23 (b)

The second half of the WIDE spreadsheet

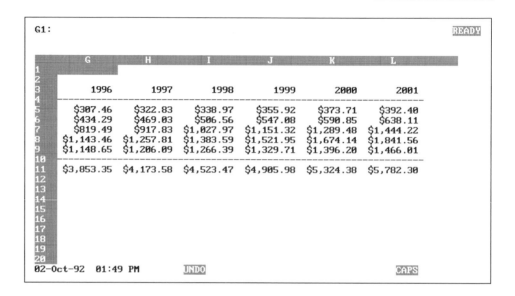

Perform the following steps to create this spreadsheet:

a. Type the text and dashes into column A. Type your name into cell D1.

b. Type the numbers and dashes into column B. In cell B11, type a formula that will add the five expense amounts above it.

c. Column C contains a series of formulas that include an assumption about how much each expense amount will increase each year. Type the following formulas and underlines into column C (note: the symbol for multiplication is *):

Move to Cell	TYPE:
C3	1+B3
C4	\-
C5	1.05*B5
C6	1.08*B6
C7	1.12*B7
C8	1.1*B8
C9	1.05*B9
C10	\-
C11	@SUM(C5..C9)

d. Save this partially completed spreadsheet onto the Advantage Diskette as WIDE.

e. Copy the formulas in the range C3..C11 into the range C3..L11. Note how quickly Lotus calculated all the answers. Imagine if you had to type each of those formulas individually; the COPY command saved you a tremendous amount of time.

f. Format the entire spreadsheet in the currency format to two decimal places.

g. Globally widen each of the columns in this spreadsheet to 12.

   h. Format the range B3..L3 in the fixed format to zero decimal places.

   i. Save the spreadsheet again onto your Advantage Diskette as WIDE.

   j. Practice changing a few numbers in the range B5..B9. Note how quickly Lotus 1-2-3 can recalculate the spreadsheet.

   k. Print the spreadsheet in both the as-displayed and cell-formulas formats. Include the current date in a header.

4. Clear RAM of any spreadsheet data after making sure you have saved your work. Perform the following steps to create the spreadsheet in Figure 3.24.

Figure 3.24

The PRACTICE
spreadsheet

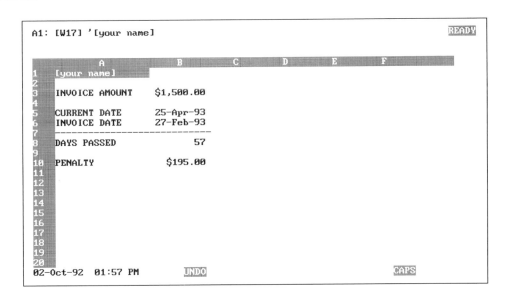

   a. Type the following text into the appropriate cells:

Move to Cell	TYPE:
A1	[your name]
A3	INVOICE AMOUNT
A5	CURRENT DATE
A6	INVOICE DATE
A7	\-
A8	DAYS PASSED
A10	PENALTY
B7	\-

   b. Widen column A to 17.

   c. Type the invoice amount of 1500 into cell B3.

   d. Type the current date of @DATE(93,4,25) into cell B5. Format the range B5..B6 in the date format. (Note: You may have to widen column B.)

   e. Type the invoice date of @DATE(93,2,27) into cell B6.

f.   Type a formula into cell A8 to calculate the number of days that have passed since the invoice was sent.

g.   Type a formula into cell B10 that does the following: If the number of days that have passed is greater than 30, calculate a 13% penalty (based on the invoice amount). Otherwise don't calculate a penalty.

h.   Format cells B3 and B10 in the currency format to two decimal places.

i.   Save this spreadsheet onto the Advantage Diskette as PRACTICE.

j.   Print this spreadsheet in both the as-displayed and cell-formulas formats.

5.   Retrieve EMPLOYEE from the Advantage Diskette (Figure 3.25). Perform the following steps:

Figure 3.25

The EMPLOYEE spreadsheet

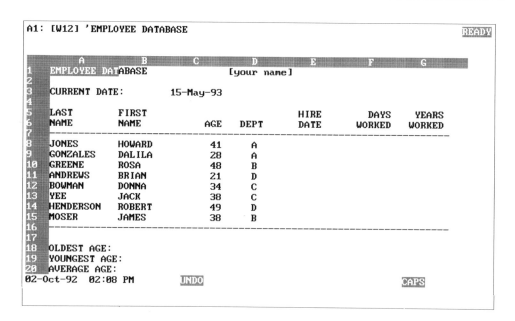

a.   Using the @DATE function, type the following dates into column E (remember to use the @DATE function when typing in the italicized dates):

Move to Cell	TYPE:
E8	*April 15, 1969*
E9	*May 11, 1984*
E10	*March 16, 1973*
E11	*January 15, 1988*
E12	*July 20, 1979*
E13	*February 15, 1980*
E14	*June 1, 1974*
E15	*November 10, 1981*

b. Include a formula in cell F8 that subtracts the Hire Date from the Current Date to determine the number of days worked. (Note: You may need to include an absolute reference.)

c. Copy the formula in cell F8 into the seven cells below it.

d. Include a formula in cell G8 that divides cell F8 by 365 to determine the number of years worked.

e. Copy this formula into the seven cells below G8.

f. Type formulas into the range C18..C20 that calculate the oldest, youngest, and average ages.

g. Type your name into cell D1.

h. Save this spreadsheet onto the Advantage Diskette as EMPLOYEE.

i. Print the EMPLOYEE spreadsheet in both the as-displayed and cell-formulas formats.

6. Retrieve the file called CIRC from the Advantage Diskette. Correct all the circular references in the spreadsheet. Type your name into cell A1. Save the spreadsheet. Print the spreadsheet in the as-displayed format.

SESSION 4

LOTUS 1-2-3:
MANAGING A SPREADSHEET

What you have done so far with spreadsheets is sophisticated enough. Now we show you some even more sophisticated commands: freezing titles on the screen, using a window to see both sides of a spreadsheet, protecting important cells from inadvertent changes, and using macros—commands that simplify commands.

PREVIEW

When you have completed this session, you will be able to:

Use range names.
·
Freeze titles on the screen.
·
Use a window to see both sides of a large spreadsheet.
·
Protect the cells in your spreadsheet that contain formulas.
·
Perform a consolidation procedure.
·
Use the file-linking capability.
·
Describe what macros are and why they're important.
·
Create save and print macros.
·

Why Is This Session Important?
Range Names
Titles
       Setting Titles
       Clearing Titles
Windows
       Creating and Using a Window
       Clearing the Window
Protection
Consolidating Spreadsheets
File-Linking (Version 2.2)
What Is a Macro?
Creating Macros
       Creating a Save Macro
       Creating Print Macros
       Documenting Your Macros
Creating Macros Using Learn Mode
       Creating a Save Macro
       Creating Print Macros
       Documenting Your Macros
Other Useful Macros
Summary
       Command Summary
Key Terms
Exercises
       Short Answer
       Hands-On

WHY IS THIS SESSION IMPORTANT?

Once you have created a spreadsheet, you need to know how to manage it—that is, how to protect it, maintain it, and take advantage of its flexibility. This session shows you some techniques for managing the spreadsheets you create through the use of titles, windows, protection, consolidation procedures, file-linking, and macros.

Before proceeding, make sure the following are true:

1. You have loaded Lotus 1-2-3 and are displaying an empty spreadsheet template on the screen.

2. Your Advantage Diskette is inserted in the drive. You will save your work onto the diskette and retrieve the files that have been created for you. (Note: The Advantage Diskette can be made by copying all the files off the instructor's Master Advantage Diskette onto a formatted diskette.)

RANGE NAMES

Lotus 1-2-3 provides you with the capability to give a name to a range of cells, which makes your spreadsheets easier to create and to use. In this section you will retrieve a file named YEAR (Figure 4.1) from the Advantage Diskette so that you can practice using the **RANGE NAME CREATE** command. You will give the name EXPENSES to the range B12..E12 (quarterly expense totals) and then use this name while determining the average, minimum, and maximum quarterly expense totals. Most users find it easier to use **range names,** such as the name EXPENSES, rather than actual cell references, such as B12..E12.

Range names can be up to 15 characters of any combination of letters and numbers. However, don't begin a range name with a number or include any spaces. In addition, don't use range names that are also cell addresses, such as T10.

Perform the following steps:

1. Retrieve the file named YEAR from the Advantage Diskette. (The procedure for retrieving was described in Session 2.)

2. Position the cursor on cell B12, which is the beginning of the range you want to name.

Figure 4.1

The YEAR
spreadsheet

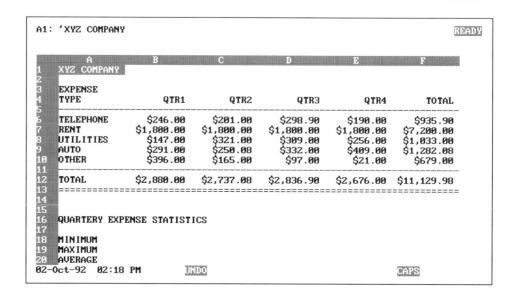

3. TYPE: /
    CHOOSE: Range, Name, Create

4. Lotus is now waiting for you to type in a range name.
    TYPE: EXPENSES
    PRESS: (Enter)

6. PRESS: (→) *to highlight the range B12..E12*
    PRESS: (Enter)
    The spreadsheet should again be in Ready mode.

7. To see how you can use the name EXPENSES in a formula, position the
    cursor in cell B18.
    TYPE: @MIN(EXPENSES)
    PRESS: (Enter)

8. With the cursor in cell B19:
    TYPE: @MAX(EXPENSES)
    PRESS: (Enter)

9. With the cursor in cell B20:
    TYPE: @AVG(EXPENSES)
    PRESS: (Enter)
    The spreadsheet should look like Figure 4.2.

Figure 4.2

The @MIN, @MAX, and @AVG functions have been included in the YEAR spreadsheet.

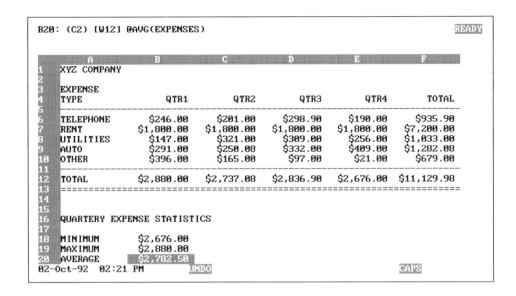

10. Save this spreadsheet as YEAR onto the Advantage Diskette.

You will use the RANGE NAME CREATE command in this session when we lead you through consolidating data. You will also use this command when we lead you through creating macros.

Quick Reference

Naming a Range

1. Position the cursor at the beginning of the range to be named.
2. Initiate Menu mode.
3. CHOOSE: Range, Name, Create
4. Type in a name and then press (Enter).
5. Highlight the range of cells to be named, and then press (Enter).

TITLES

In this section you will practice using the **TITLES** command with the FORECAST spreadsheet that is stored on the Advantage Diskette. This command makes it easier to manage spreadsheets that can't easily fit on the screen at once. With large spreadsheets, column and row labels, or headings, which serve as the frame of reference for the spreadsheet, typically scroll off the screen when you view other parts of the spreadsheet. The TITLES command provides you with the option of freezing (or locking) row headings, column headings, or both row and column headings on the screen. As a result, you can scroll the screen to view other parts of a large spreadsheet, while keeping headings text on the screen.

The FORECAST spreadsheet forecasts expenses for 10 years; starting with 1991. (Note: If you want to create this spreadsheet yourself, the instructions are included as a hands-on exercise in Session 3. The spreadsheet is named WIDE.) The expenses for 1991 were typed into the range B5..B9. The range C5..C9 contains formulas that calculate the percentage increase for each expense type. Cell C11 totals the expense amounts in the range C5..C9. The formulas in column C were copied through column L.

SETTING TITLES

Perform the following steps to set vertical titles—that is, labels in a column that identify the rows—using the TITLES command:

1. Retrieve a copy of the FORECAST spreadsheet from the Advantage Diskette. (The procedure for retrieving was described in Session 2.)

2. The cursor should be positioned in cell A1. The screen should look like Figure 4.3.

Figure 4.3

The screen after retrieving the FORECAST spreadsheet

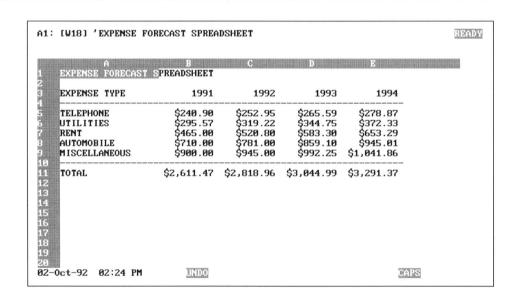

```
A1: [W18] 'EXPENSE FORECAST SPREADSHEET                                   READY

              A              B           C           D           E
1    EXPENSE FORECAST SPREADSHEET
2
3    EXPENSE TYPE          1991        1992        1993        1994
4    ------------------------------------------------------------------
5    TELEPHONE           $240.90     $252.95     $265.59     $278.87
6    UTILITIES           $295.57     $319.22     $344.75     $372.33
7    RENT                $465.00     $520.80     $583.30     $653.29
8    AUTOMOBILE          $710.00     $781.00     $859.10     $945.01
9    MISCELLANEOUS       $900.00     $945.00     $992.25   $1,041.86
10   ------------------------------------------------------------------
11   TOTAL             $2,611.47   $2,818.96   $3,044.99   $3,291.37
12
13
14
15
16
17
18
19
20
02-Oct-92   02:24 PM            UNDO                          CAPS
```

PRESS: → *seven times*

The screen should look like Figure 4.4. Note that the row headings in column A have scrolled off the screen to the left. The text in column A provides a frame of reference for the spreadsheet; it would be useful if this information would always remain on the screen no matter what cell the cursor is positioned in. To accomplish this, you must use the TITLES command.

Figure 4.4

The FORECAST spreadsheet after pressing → seven times. Note that the column headings in column A have scrolled off the screen to the left.

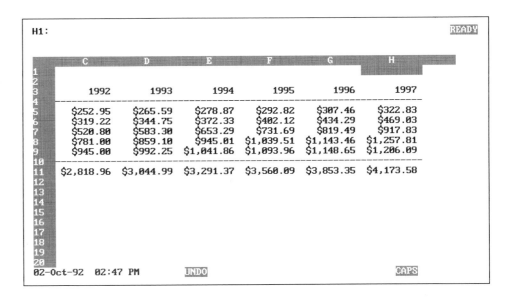

3. In the steps below you will freeze the headings in column A on the screen.
   PRESS: [Home]
   PRESS: [→]

4. The cursor is now positioned in column B to the right of the text that you want to freeze on the screen.
   TYPE: /
   CHOOSE: Worksheet, Titles

5. To freeze the titles that are positioned vertically in column A:
   CHOOSE: Vertical

6. The spreadsheet should again be in Ready mode. To see if the titles in column A are frozen in place:
   PRESS: [→] *until you can see column L on the screen*
   Note that the text in column A has remained frozen on the screen (Figure 4.5).

7. To see what happens when you press [Home]:
   PRESS: [Home]
   Note that because the TITLES command is in effect, you can't move the cursor into column A.

You use the same steps to save horizontal labels, except you choose Horizontal after choosing Worksheet, Titles. If you wish, you can freeze both horizontal and vertical labels by choosing Both.

Figure 4.5

After freezing titles,
the headings in
column A remain
on the screen
even after press-
ing [→].

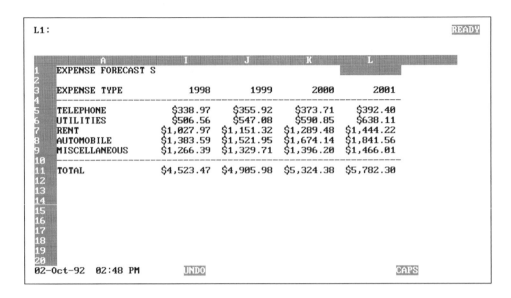

Quick Reference   1.   Position the cursor to the right of the row headings and/or below the
                              column headings that you want to freeze.
Setting Titles   2.   Initiate Menu mode (/).
                         3.   CHOOSE: Worksheet, Titles
                         4.   Choose the Both, Horizontal, or Vertical option.

CLEARING TITLES

The cursor should be positioned in cell B1. If you decide you need to make
changes to the contents of column A you will need to "unfreeze" the column A
titles. Perform the following steps to clear the titles:

1.   TYPE: /
     CHOOSE: Worksheet, Titles, Clear

2.   PRESS: [Home]
     The cursor should have jumped to cell A1.

Quick Reference   1.   Initiate Menu mode.
Clearing Titles   2.   CHOOSE: Worksheet, Titles, Clear

WINDOWS

Using the **WINDOW** command enables you to see both sides of a wide spreadsheet, or both the top and bottom of a long spreadsheet. You will practice using this command with the FORECAST spreadsheet. You will create a window that enables you to see columns A and B on the left and columns J, K, and L on the right. The [F6] **(Window) key** is used to move the cursor from the left side of the window to the right side of the window, and vice versa. Before using the WINDOW command, first position the cursor in column C (the column to the right of the columns you want on the left side of the window).

CREATING AND USING A WINDOW

1. If you haven't done so already, retrieve a copy of the FORECAST spreadsheet from the Advantage Diskette.

2. Position the cursor in column C. *The cursor is strategically positioned to the right of what you want to remain on the left side of the window.*

3. TYPE: /
   CHOOSE: Worksheet, Window

4. To set a vertical window:
   CHOOSE: Vertical
   The screen should look like Figure 4.6.

Figure 4.6

Vertical window. After creating a window, press [F6] to move the cursor from one window to another.

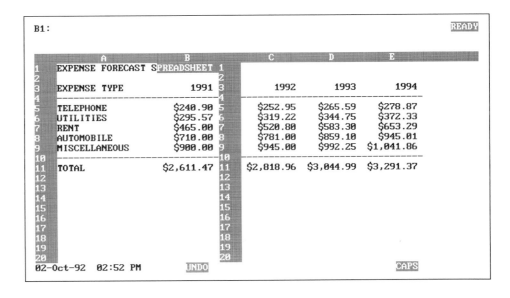

5. The cursor is positioned on the left side of the window. To position the cursor on the right side of the window:
    PRESS: [F6]

6. Position the cursor in column L.
    The screen should look like Figure 4.7. Note that you can now see both sides of the FORECAST spreadsheet. With both sides of the spreadsheet visible on the screen, you can see how a change in a 1991 expense amount affects the 2001 expense amounts.

Figure 4.7

The WORKSHEET WINDOW command is useful if you want to see both ends of a very wide or very long spreadsheet. Note that you can see both ends of this wide spreadsheet.

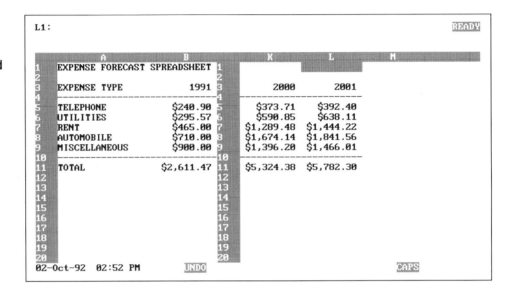

7. To switch back to the left side of the window:
    PRESS: [F6]
    The cursor should still be in cell B1.

8. To see how a change in one of the 1991 expense amounts affects the 2001 expense amounts, first position the cursor on cell B5 (1991's Telephone expense amount). You can see that the telephone expense for 2001 (L5) is $392.40.

9. TYPE: 425
    PRESS: [Enter]
    L5 now says $692.28. You can see how a change in the 1991 Telephone amount affects the 2001 amount.

10. Press [F6] a few times to see how the cursor switches windows.

1. Position the cursor to the right of the columns you want to remain on the left side of the window or below the rows you want to remain on the top of the window.
2. Initiate Menu mode.
3. CHOOSE: Worksheet, Window
4. Choose the Horizontal or Vertical option. To switch between windows, press F6.

CLEARING THE WINDOW

To clear the window you have created, perform the following steps:

1. TYPE: /

2. CHOOSE: Worksheet, Window, Clear
   The window should have disappeared from the spreadsheet. Press F6, and you see that nothing happens.

1. Initiate Menu mode.
2. CHOOSE: Worksheet, Window, Clear

PROTECTION

In this section you will practice protecting the cells in the FORECAST spreadsheet that contain formulas so that you can't accidentally change them. For example, you could wipe out any cell that contains a formula by simply positioning the cursor on it and then typing something into the cell. What you type will replace the formula. (The only cells that you might want to change are the 1991 expense amounts so that you can see how a change in them affects the totals in future years.) You use two commands to protect a spreadsheet:

1. First the GLOBAL command to protect the entire spreadsheet.

2. Then use the RANGE UNPROTECT command to "unprotect" the cells into which you will enter data or which you'll possibly change. Before using this command, you will position the cursor at the beginning of the range you want to unprotect.

To globally protect the entire spreadsheet, perform the following steps:

1. TYPE: /
    CHOOSE: Worksheet, Global, Protection

2. To enable protection:
    CHOOSE: Enable
    Every cell in this spreadsheet is now protected.

3. To see if every cell is protected, position the cursor in cell B5.
    TYPE: 260
    PRESS: [Enter]

4. A message should be displaying in the bottom-left of the screen that informs
    you that cell B5 is protected. To return to Ready mode:
    PRESS: [Esc]

To unprotect the range B5..B9, perform the following steps:

1. Position the cursor on cell B5.

2. TYPE: /
    CHOOSE: Range, Unprotect

3. Lotus 1-2-3 now wants to know what range of cells to unprotect.
    PRESS: [↓] *to highlight the range B5..B9*
    PRESS: [Enter]

If you are using a color monitor, the range B5..B9 should appear in a different
color. If you are using a monochrome monitor, the range B5..B9 should appear in
a slightly different shade.

You can now type numbers into the range B5..B9 without risk of wiping out any
of the text or formulas in the spreadsheet.

....

Quick Reference   To globally protect the entire spreadsheet:
                            1. Initiate Menu mode.
Protection   2. CHOOSE: Worksheet, Global, Protection, Enable

                            To unprotect a range of cells so it can be altered:
                            1. TYPE: /
                            2. CHOOSE: Range, Unprotect
                            3. Highlight the range of cells to be unprotected, and then press [Enter].

....

CONSOLIDATING SPREADSHEETS

In this section you learn how to add data from four different spreadsheets to data in designated cells in a summary spreadsheet. The procedure you use to combine data from different spreadsheets is referred to as a **consolidation procedure**. When consolidating, Lotus will ask whether you want to copy, add, or subtract the data from another spreadsheet. If you choose to *copy* from another (source) spreadsheet, the *formulas* contained in the source spreadsheet are copied into the current (target) spreadsheet. Choosing the *add* or *subtract* options will bring just the data (or formula results) into the target spreadsheet. Then, depending on the option you choose the source data will be added or subtracted from the target cell. In this section you will use the Add option.

The files you will work with are stored on the Advantage Diskette. The target file into which you will consolidate source data is called SUMMARY (Figure 4.8). We want to use source data from four quarterly spreadsheets (called Q1, Q2, Q3, and Q4). Q1 is shown in Figure 4.9. The other three spreadsheets are almost identical, except the headings reflect different months and the expense data is slightly different. You will consolidate the totals in the range E4..E8 from each of the quarterly spreadsheets into the SUMMARY spreadsheet.

Figure 4.8

The SUMMARY spreadsheet. The expense data for this spreadsheet will be added from four quarterly spreadsheets using a consolidation procedure.

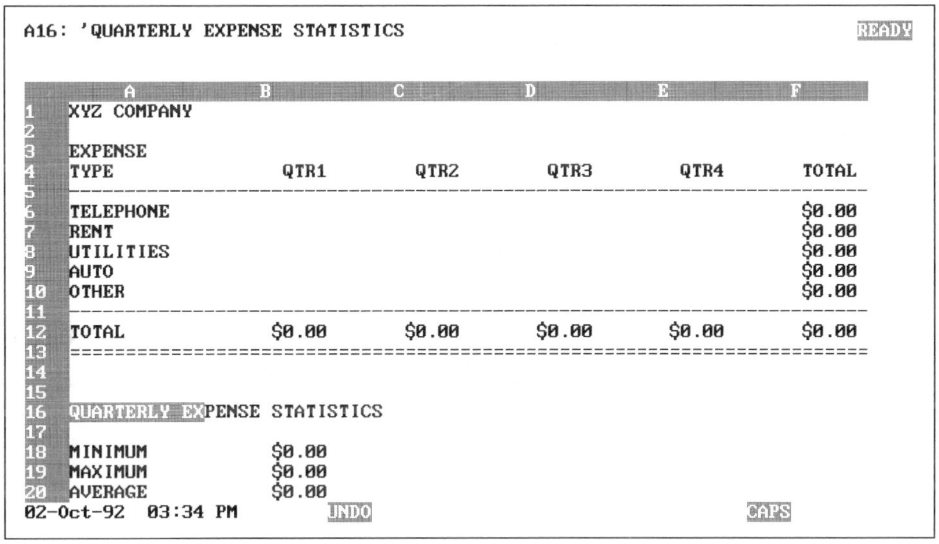

Figure 4.9

The Q1 spread-
sheet. The range
E4..E8 has been
named Totals
using the RANGE
NAME command.

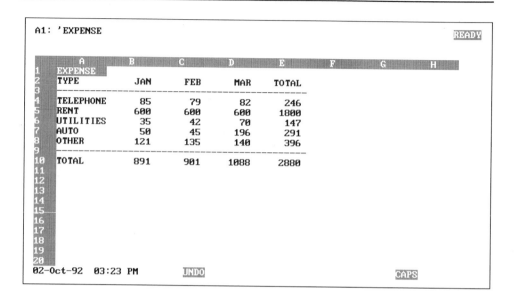

The range name of Totals has been given to the range E4..E8 in each of the
quarterly spreadsheets. Calculations will be performed in the SUMMARY
spreadsheet that determine yearly expense totals, percentages, and statistics. The
totals from the Q1 spreadsheet will be added to the range B6..B10 in the
SUMMARY spreadsheet. The totals from the Q2 spreadsheet will be added to the
range C6..C10 in the SUMMARY spreadsheet, and so on. Before beginning the
consolidation procedure, you must retrieve a copy of the spreadsheet that you will
consolidate into. *Then you must always position the cursor where you want the
consolidated data to appear.*

Perform the following steps to consolidate the totals from the four quarterly
spreadsheets into the SUMMARY spreadsheet:

1. Retrieve a copy of the SUMMARY spreadsheet. (The procedure for retrieving
    was described in Session 2.)

2. Position the cursor in cell B6 (TELEPHONE)—this is where you want the Q1
    totals to be positioned.

3. TYPE: /
    CHOOSE: File, Combine

4. Lotus 1-2-3 is now giving you the option of copying the cell contents from the
    source spreadsheet (for example, the formulas) or adding or subtracting the
    source numbers to or from the numbers in the target cells.
    CHOOSE: Add

5. Lotus 1-2-3 now wants to know whether you want to add the data from an entire spreadsheet or from a named or specified range of cells. To bring data in from a named range (TOTALS):
   CHOOSE: Named/Specified-Range

6. To specify the name of the range you want to add:
   TYPE: TOTALS
   PRESS: (Enter)

7. You must now specify from which file you want to bring the data. If the files on the Advantage Diskette are listed on the screen, highlight Q1 and press (Enter). Otherwise:
   TYPE: A:Q1
   PRESS: (Enter)
   The screen should look like Figure 4.10.

Figure 4.10

The Totals range from the Q1 spreadsheet has been added to the SUMMARY spreadsheet.

```
B6: (G) [W12] 246                                              READY

          A          B          C          D          E          F
 1   XYZ COMPANY
 2
 3   EXPENSE
 4   TYPE          QTR1       QTR2       QTR3       QTR4       TOTAL
 5   ----------------------------------------------------------------
 6   TELEPHONE      246                                       $246.00
 7   RENT          1800                                     $1,800.00
 8   UTILITIES      147                                       $147.00
 9   AUTO           291                                       $291.00
10   OTHER          396                                       $396.00
11   ----------------------------------------------------------------
12   TOTAL      $2,880.00     $0.00      $0.00      $0.00  $2,880.00
13   ================================================================
14
15
16   QUARTERLY EXPENSE STATISTICS
17
18   MINIMUM         $0.00
19   MAXIMUM     $2,880.00
20   AVERAGE       $720.00
02-Oct-92  03:44 PM          UNDO                          CAPS
```

---

8. Consolidate the totals from the Q2, Q3, and Q4 spreadsheets. The procedure is almost identical to the procedure you used to consolidate the totals from the Q1 spreadsheet.

   Make sure to position the cursor in the appropriate cell before initiating the consolidation procedure:

   a. Position the cursor in cell C6 before consolidating from the Q2 file.
   b. Position the cursor in cell D6 before consolidating from the Q3 file.
   c. Position the cursor in cell E6 before consolidating from the Q4 file.

   When you are finished consolidating for the four quarters, the screen should look like Figure 4.11.

Figure 4.11

The Totals range from the Q2, Q3, and Q4 spreadsheets has been added to the SUMMARY spreadsheet.

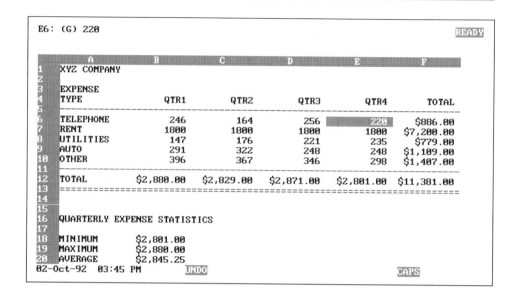

9. *Don't* save the SUMMARY spreadsheet onto your data diskette. You'll be using the previous version of this spreadsheet in the next section on File-Linking.

Quick Reference

Consolidating Spreadsheets

1. Position the cursor in the target cell you want data to be consolidated into.
2. Initiate Menu mode.
3. CHOOSE: File, Combine
4. Choose the Add, Subtract, or Copy option.
5. Choose the Named/Specified-Range option.
6. Specify the cell or range of cells to be consolidated.
7. Highlight the name of the source file you want to consolidate data from, and then press (Enter).

FILE-LINKING (VERSION 2.2)

(Note: If you are using Lotus 1-2-3, version 2.01, proceed to the next section on macros.) Lotus 1-2-3 provides users with the ability to put formulas that refer to cells in spreadsheets stored on disk into cells in the spreadsheet that is displayed on the screen (and stored in RAM). Later changes made to the files stored on disk will also be reflected in the target spreadsheet, which contains the linking formulas. This capability, referred to as **file-linking**, makes it easier to consolidate data than does the consolidation procedure described in the last section.

In the following steps you will retrieve the SUMMARY (target) spreadsheet and put linking formulas in it that refer to the Totals range E4..E8 in the Q1, Q2, Q3, and Q4 (source) spreadsheets. Figure 4.12 shows the linking formulas for Q1, Q2, and Q3 that you will put into the SUMMARY spreadsheet.

Figure 4.12

These linking formulas will be put into the SUMMARY spreadsheet (the QTR4 column has scrolled off the screen to the right).

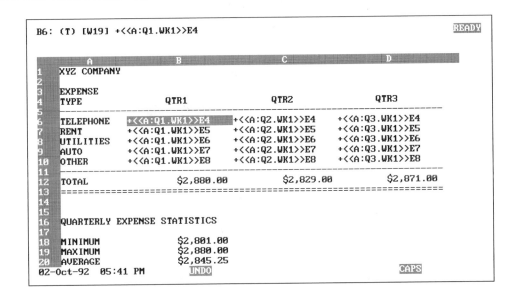

```
B6: (T) [W19] +<<A:Q1.WK1>>E4                                    READY

        A              B              C              D
 1 XYZ COMPANY
 2
 3 EXPENSE
 4 TYPE           QTR1           QTR2           QTR3
 5  ─────────────────────────────────────────────────────────────
 6 TELEPHONE    +<<A:Q1.WK1>>E4  +<<A:Q2.WK1>>E4  +<<A:Q3.WK1>>E4
 7 RENT         +<<A:Q1.WK1>>E5  +<<A:Q2.WK1>>E5  +<<A:Q3.WK1>>E5
 8 UTILITIES    +<<A:Q1.WK1>>E6  +<<A:Q2.WK1>>E6  +<<A:Q3.WK1>>E6
 9 AUTO         +<<A:Q1.WK1>>E7  +<<A:Q2.WK1>>E7  +<<A:Q3.WK1>>E7
10 OTHER        +<<A:Q1.WK1>>E8  +<<A:Q2.WK1>>E8  +<<A:Q3.WK1>>E8
11  ─────────────────────────────────────────────────────────────
12 TOTAL          $2,880.00       $2,829.00       $2,871.00
13  ═══════════════════════════════════════════════════════════════
14
15
16 QUARTERLY EXPENSE STATISTICS
17
18 MINIMUM        $2,801.00
19 MAXIMUM        $2,880.00
20 AVERAGE        $2,845.25
02-Oct-92  05:41 PM        UNDO                         CAPS
```

Perform the following steps (when you are done, your screen should look like Figure 4.11):

1. Retrieve the original version of SUMMARY from the Advantage Diskette. Or, in the new version of SUMMARY that you prepared in the last section, erase the range B6..E10 using the RANGE ERASE command.

2. To establish a link to the Q1 file, first position the cursor in cell B6. (Remember, your Advantage Diskette is designated by A:.)

3. TYPE: +<<A:Q1>>E4
   PRESS: (Enter)
   The first quarter Telephone expense amount (246) should be displaying in cell B6 (see Figure 4.11).

4. The cursor should be positioned in cell B6. Now copy this formula down into the four cells below:
   TYPE: /
   CHOOSE: Copy
   Since the cursor is positioned on the cell you're copying from (B6):
   PRESS: (Enter)

To highlight the range you're copying to (the four cells below), you must first anchor the beginning of the range:

TYPE: .

PRESS: ⬇ *four times*

PRESS: Enter

Note that the formula in cell B6 adjusted downward—that is, the formula in cell B7 is +<<A:Q1>>E5, the formula in cell B8 is +<<A:Q1>>E6, and so on.

5. Now type a formula in cell C6 that refers to the Q2 totals (+<<A:Q2>>E4), and then copy it down into the four cells below.

6. Type a formula in cell D6 that refers to the Q3 totals (+<<A:Q3>>E4) and then copy it down into the four cells below.

7. And finally, type a formula in cell E6 that refers to the Q4 totals (+<<A:Q4>>E4) and then copy it down into the four cells below. Your spreadsheet should look like Figure 4.11.

8. Save the SUMMARY spreadsheet onto the Advantage Diskette. *If any changes are made in the Q1, Q2, Q3, or Q4 file, they will now be reflected automatically in the SUMMARY file.*

....

Quick Reference   To establish a link between the target spreadsheet in RAM and a source file
                             saved on the disk, position the cursor in a target cell and then use the
File-Linking   following formula:

                                 +<<drive designation:filename>>cell reference

                             For example, to add data from cell B5 in a spreadsheet named INCOME that
                             is stored on a diskette in drive A:, type:

                                 +<<A:INCOME>>B5

....

WHAT IS A MACRO?

Wouldn't it be convenient to press only two keys to print your spreadsheet? Or to press two keys to consolidate all the data from your detail (subsidiary) spreadsheets into your summary spreadsheet? Or to press two keys to save your spreadsheet onto your diskette? This session teaches you how to use macros to automate procedures, which can save you time and help ensure the reliability of procedures.

A **macro** is a sequence of keystrokes that have been typed into a cell or cells outside the normal print range—that is, outside of the range of columns and rows that are normally printed out. Once the keystrokes have been entered as a macro, the name of the macro is used as a shortcut to execute the command whose keystrokes it represents. In other words, performing a procedure using a macro involves pressing only two keys, whereas performing the same procedure without a macro can involve pressing many keys. For example, when saving a spreadsheet you must press the following keys:

1. The forward slash key (/), which takes you into Menu mode.
2. The letter F, which initiates the FILE group of commands.
3. The letter S, which initiates the SAVE command.
4. The name of the file (if you're saving it for the first time).
5. (Enter), which executes the SAVE command.
6. If you have already saved the file once, you will also have to press the letter R, which replaces the copy on disk with the contents of RAM.

Using a macro to save your spreadsheet will do more than just save your spreadsheet—it will also save time.

Macros are stored within the current spreadsheet (on screen) and typically are used only with that spreadsheet; however, in Session 6, we describe the Macro Library Manager add-in, which allows you to use the same macros with different spreadsheets. By using macros:

- You are making the spreadsheet easier to use. Instead of having to remember all the different keystrokes required to perform a procedure, you have to remember only two keystrokes.

- You are making the spreadsheet easier to use for someone else who isn't familiar with using a spreadsheet because the new user needs to only type two keys to perform lengthy procedures.

CREATING MACROS

The steps for creating a macro include:

1. Perform manually the procedure you want to automate and write the keystrokes down on a piece of paper. To symbolize pressing (Enter), put a tilde (~) in your notes.

2. Type these keystrokes as a label into a range of cells outside the normal print range. You must precede the keystrokes with an apostrophe ('), otherwise you will never be able to get forward slash (/) into a cell because Lotus 1-2-3 will always go into Menu mode. It doesn't matter whether you use upper- or lowercase letters; however, for purposes of clarity, this session uses lowercase

letters for all keystrokes that refer to command keystrokes and uppercase letters for all keystrokes that signify either a disk drive designation (such as "B:") or a filename.

3. Name the cell the keystrokes are in. Macro keystrokes can be named in one of two ways. First, you can name a macro with a backslash (\) followed by one other character. Second, you can name a macro with up to 15 characters (this second method of naming macros is available only in version 2.2 of Lotus). The way you choose to name the macro determines how you execute the macro (described in the next step).

4. If you named the macro with a backslash and one other character, to execute the macro you must hold (Alt) down and tap the "other" character. Otherwise, you must use the RUN command ((Alt)+(F3)) to execute the macro—after initiating the RUN command, highlight the name of the macro you want to execute.

You will practice these four steps in the following section.

CREATING A SAVE MACRO

In this section you'll learn how to automate the save procedure for the spreadsheet named INCOME, which is stored on the Advantage Diskette. (You worked with the INCOME file in Session 3.) This save macro will save and replace the INCOME spreadsheet on the Advantage Diskette.

Perform the following steps to create a save macro:

1. Retrieve a copy of the INCOME spreadsheet from the Advantage Diskette. (The procedure for retrieving was described in Session 2.)

2. The first step is to save the file called INCOME manually onto the Advantage Diskette and write the keystrokes down. (Note: In macros, Lotus uses the tilde symbol to represent pressing (Enter)). You should have written the following keystrokes:
    /fs~r

3. The next step in creating a macro is to type the keystrokes into a cell, or cells, outside the normal print range (such as in column AA). Many users put their macros in column AA because it is a safe location, away from the spreadsheet model. Position the cursor in cell AA3.

4. The cursor should be positioned in cell AA3. (Be sure to type an apostrophe before the keystrokes):
   TYPE: `'/fs~r`
   PRESS: (Enter)
   The screen should look like Figure 4.13.

Figure 4.13

A save macro

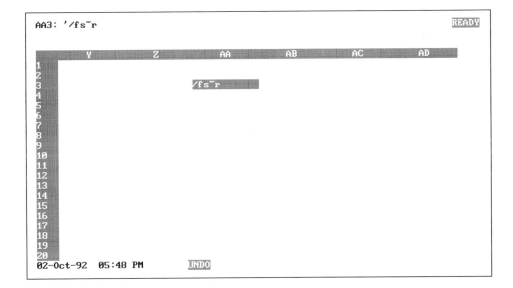

To name the keystrokes you have just entered into cell AA3, perform the following steps:

1. The cursor should be positioned on cell AA3. To enter Menu mode:
   PRESS: /

2. CHOOSE: Range, Name, Create

3. Lotus 1-2-3 is now waiting for you to type in a name for the macro. In this step you'll name the keystrokes with a backslash followed by the letter S, for Save.
   TYPE: `\s`
   PRESS: (Enter)

4. The cursor is positioned on the cell you want to name.
   PRESS: (Enter)

Since you named the keystrokes with a backslash followed by the letter S, perform the following procedure to execute the macro:

1. Hold (Alt) down and type S.

2. The INCOME file has been saved onto the Advantage Diskette.

---

1. Perform the procedure manually and write the keystrokes down. Use a tilde (~) to represent (Enter).
2. Type the keystrokes (preceded by an apostrophe) into a cell outside the normal print range (such as column AA).
3. Name the cell with either a backslash followed by one other character or, in version 2.2, with up to 15 characters.
    a. Initiate Menu mode (/)
    b. CHOOSE: Range, Name, Create
    c. TYPE: *the macro name*
    d. PRESS: (Enter)
4. If you named the macro with a backslash and one other character, to execute the macro you must hold (Alt) down and tap the "other" character. Otherwise, you must use the RUN command ((Alt)+(F3)) to execute the macro (version 2.2).

CREATING PRINT MACROS

The print procedure can often be time consuming—especially if you have to change margins or page length or add a header and a footer. Therefore, many people use print macros to automate the print procedure. In this section, you will create two print macros in the INCOME spreadsheet. The first will print your spreadsheet in the as-displayed format (which is your report, or what you see on the screen) and the second will print your spreadsheet in the cell-formulas format (which lists your program specifications, or the contents of every cell in your spreadsheet, including formulas). (You performed both of these procedures manually in Session 2.)

To create a macro that will print your spreadsheet in the as-displayed format:

1. Manually perform the procedure to print the INCOME spreadsheet in the as-displayed format and write the keystrokes down (don't include in your print range the cells that contain macro keystrokes because you wouldn't want to include them in a report). You should have written the following keystrokes down (remember: the tilde represents pressing (Enter)):
    /pprA1..G25~ooaqagpq

2. Type these keystrokes into cell AA6. Remember to precede the keystrokes with an apostrophe, and then press Enter. The screen should look like Figure 4.14.

Figure 4.14

An as-displayed print macro

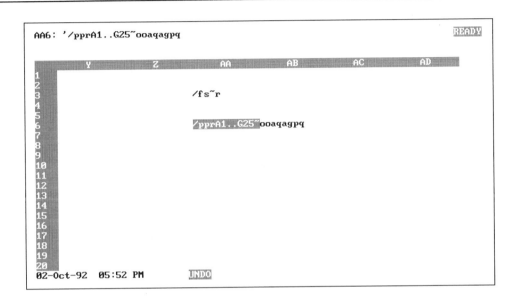

3. Using the procedure described in the previous section that describes naming a save macro (Range, Name, Create), name cell AA6 with a backslash (\ ) and the letter P, or, if you have version 2.2, name it with the name PRINT.

4. Turn the printer on. To execute the macro: (a) if you named it with a backslash followed by the letter P, hold down Alt and type P; (b) if you named it PRINT, use the RUN command (Alt+F3).

5. Use the save macro (Alt+S) to save this new macro in the spreadsheet.

To create and name a macro that will print your spreadsheet in the cell-formulas format:

1. Manually perform the procedure to print the INCOME spreadsheet in the cell-formulas format and write the keystrokes down (don't include in your print range the cells that contain macro keystrokes because you wouldn't want to include them in a report). You should have written the following keystrokes down (remember: the tilde represents pressing Enter):
   /pprA1..G25~oocqagpq

2. Key these keystrokes into cell AA9. The screen should look like Figure 4.15.

Figure 4.15

A cell-formulas
print macro

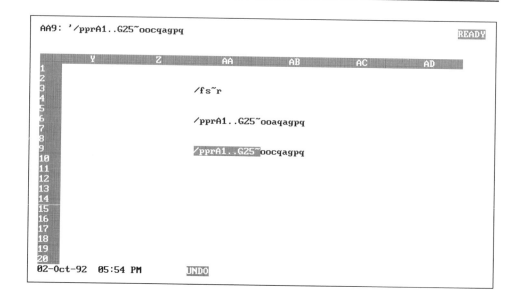

3. Name the keystrokes with a backslash (\ ) and the letter C, or name them CELLS.

4. Turn the printer on. To execute the macro: (a) if you named it with a backslash followed by the letter C, hold down [Alt] and type C; (b) if you named it CELLS, use the RUN command ([Alt]+[F3]).

5. Make sure to use the save macro ([Alt]+S) to save this new macro in the spreadsheet.

DOCUMENTING YOUR MACROS

You now have three macros in this spreadsheet. Figure 4.16 shows the three macros in column AA. For documentation, text has been typed into columns Z and AB. Column Z lists the names of the macros (for example, S, P, C); this column is useful because after you have created a number of macros, you may forget what you named a particular macro. Column AB provides a brief description of the function of each.

Note: If you are using version 2.01, skip the section on "Creating Macros Using Learn Mode." These versions don't provide the Learn capability. Resume your work in the section on "Other Useful Macros."

Figure 4.16

Macro documentation. It's a good idea to document your macros, because as more macros are added to a spreadsheet, it's easy to forget what you've named your macros and what they do.

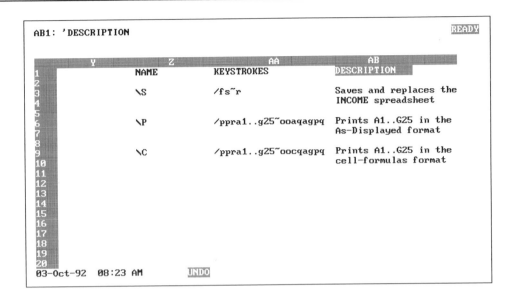

CREATING MACROS USING LEARN MODE

Version 2.2 of Lotus 1-2-3 includes the **LEARN** command. This command makes it easier to create macros because Lotus automatically records the keystrokes you want to automate in a range of cells that you define. Since Lotus supplies the keystrokes for you, data entry errors are minimized. The steps required to use the Learn feature include:

1. Specify the Learn range using the WORKSHEET LEARN RANGE command. Your keystrokes are automatically recorded in the range you define.

2. Initiate the LEARN command ((Alt)+(F5)) and perform the procedure you want to automate.

3. When you have completed the procedure you want to automate, turn the LEARN command off ((Alt)+(F5)).

4. Name the range the keystrokes are in (using the RANGE NAME CREATE command) with a backslash (\ ) followed by one other character. (You need to name only the first cell in the macro keystroke range, because Lotus automatically looks down the column to execute additional keystrokes. When a blank cell is encountered, the macro stops.) Lotus 1-2-3 recognizes cells named in this manner as cells that contain macro keystrokes.

5. Execute the macro keystrokes by holding down (Alt) and tapping the other character you used in the preceding step.

CREATING A SAVE MACRO

Perform the following steps using the LEARN command to create a save macro for the BILLS spreadsheet. You will put the save macro keystrokes in cell AA3.

1. Retrieve a copy of the BILLS spreadsheet from the Advantage Diskette.

2. Position the cursor in cell AA3.

3. To initiate Menu mode so you can define the learn range:
    TYPE: /
    CHOOSE: Worksheet, Learn, Range

4. The cursor is positioned at the beginning of the soon-to-be Learn range. Even though all the keystrokes necessary to perform the save procedure will fit in a few cells, you are going to include 20 cells in the Learn range because it's better to define too many cells to hold a macro's keystrokes rather than too few. If the Learn range isn't large enough, the LEARN command will halt, and you'll have an incompletely recorded macro. Twenty cells is large enough for almost any macro you create.
    To anchor the beginning of the Learn range:
    TYPE: .
    To include 20 cells in the Learn range:
    PRESS: PgDn
    The screen should look similar to Figure 4.17.

Figure 4.17

Defining a Learn range (Lotus 2.2). To define a Learn range, you must use the LEARN command. Your keystrokes are recorded in the range.

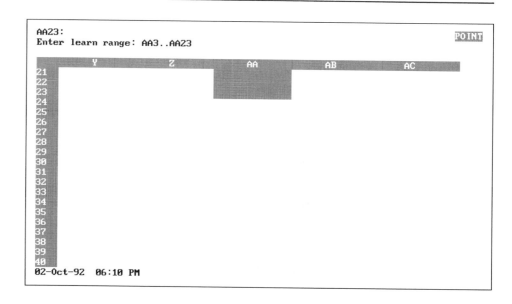

PRESS: Enter
The spreadsheet should have returned to Ready mode.

5. Now that the Learn range has been defined, it's time to activate the LEARN command and then perform the save procedure, which will automatically create a save macro. It doesn't matter where the cursor is positioned because the keystrokes will automatically record in the Learn range.

   To initiate the LEARN command:

   PRESS: Alt +F5

   "LEARN" is displaying at the bottom of the screen. Any key you press now will be recorded in the Learn range—that is, until you turn the LEARN command off. Press the following keys to record the Save procedure. (The first keystroke moves the cursor to cell A1 so that when you retrieve the spreadsheet later, the cursor will be positioned in cell A1.) *Note: When choosing commands below, be sure to choose commands by typing the first, or underlined, character of the command instead of highlighting the command and then pressing* Enter.

   PRESS: Home

   TYPE: /

   CHOOSE: File, Save

   PRESS: Enter

   CHOOSE: Replace

6. To turn the LEARN command off:

   PRESS: Alt +F5

   Note that the LEARN indicator in the bottom-center of your screen disappeared.

7. Move the cursor to column AA. You should see the keystrokes in cells AA3 and AA4 (Figure 4.18).

Figure 4.18

These save macro keystrokes were recorded in AA3..AA4 using the LEARN command.

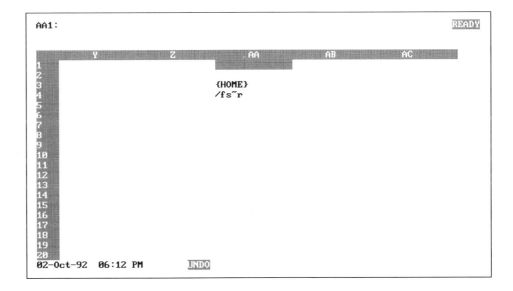

8. In this step, you will name the keystrokes you have just entered into cell AA3. The cursor should be positioned on cell AA3. To enter Menu mode:
    TYPE: /
    CHOOSE: Range, Name, Create
    Lotus 1-2-3 is now waiting for you to type in a name for the macro. Because macros are named with a backslash followed by one other character:
    TYPE: \s
    PRESS: (Enter)
    The cursor is positioned on the cell you want to name. To tell Lotus what cell(s) you want to name:
    PRESS: (Enter)
    (If macro keystrokes extend down the column—for example, cells AA4, AA5, and AA6—you still have to name only cell AA3. When executing a macro, Lotus automatically looks down the column to execute additional keystrokes that are part of the macro.)

9. To execute the save macro, hold (Alt) down and type the letter S.

The BILLS file has now been saved again onto the Advantage Diskette.

Quick Reference

Creating and Using Macros (Learn mode)

1. Initiate Menu mode.
2. CHOOSE: Worksheet, Learn
3. Highlight the Learn range and press (Enter).
4. Initiate the LEARN command ((Alt)+(F5)) and perform the procedure you want to automate.
5. When you have completed the procedure you want to automate, turn the LEARN command off ((Alt)+(F5)).
6. Name the cells with either a backslash followed by one other character or with up to 15 characters:
    Initiate Menu mode
    CHOOSE: Range, Name, Create
    TYPE: *the macro name*
    PRESS: (Enter)
7. If you named the macro with a backslash and one other character, to execute the macro you must hold (Alt) down and type the "other" character. Otherwise, you must use the RUN command ((Alt)+(F3)) to execute the macro.

CREATING PRINT MACROS

In this section, you will use the LEARN command to create two print macros in the BILLS spreadsheet. The first will print your spreadsheet in the as-displayed format (which is your report, or what you see on the screen) and the second will print your spreadsheet in the cell-formulas format (which lists your program specifications, or the contents of every cell in your spreadsheet, including formulas). The first step you perform will cancel the previous Learn range (that you defined when you created the save macro) using the WORKSHEET LEARN CANCEL command. You will then define a new Learn range.

To create a macro that prints the BILLS spreadsheet in the as-displayed format:

1. To cancel the current Learn range:
   TYPE: /
   CHOOSE: Worksheet, Learn, Cancel

2. Position the cursor in cell AA6, which marks the beginning of the new Learn range.

3. To initiate Menu mode so you can define the Learn range:
   TYPE: /
   CHOOSE: Worksheet, Learn, Range

4. The cursor is positioned at the beginning of the soon-to-be Learn range. To anchor the beginning of the Learn range:
   TYPE: .
   To include 20 cells in the Learn range:
   PRESS: [PgDn]
   PRESS: [Enter]
   The spreadsheet should have returned to Ready mode.

5. Now that the Learn range has been defined, it's time to activate the LEARN command and then perform the procedure to print the spreadsheet in the as-displayed format. It doesn't matter where the cursor is positioned because the keystrokes will automatically record in the Learn range.
   To initiate the LEARN command:
   PRESS: [Alt]+[F5]
   Any key you press will now be recorded in the Learn range—that is, until you turn the LEARN command off. (When choosing commands, remember to type the underlined character of the command option.) Press the following keys to print the spreadsheet in the as-displayed format (make sure the printer is on):
   TYPE: /
   CHOOSE: Print, Printer, Range
   TYPE: A1..G25
   PRESS: [Enter]
   CHOOSE: Options, Other, As-displayed, Quit
   CHOOSE: Align, Go, Page, Quit

6. To turn the LEARN command off:
   PRESS: [Alt]+[F5]

7. When you press one of the cursor-movement keys or [Enter], you'll see the keystrokes in cell AA6 (Figure 4.19).

8. In this step, you will name the keystrokes you have just entered into cell AA6. The cursor should be positioned on cell AA6. To enter Menu mode:
PRESS: /
CHOOSE: Range, Name, Create
Lotus 1-2-3 is now waiting for you to type in a name for the macro.
TYPE: \p
PRESS: [Enter]
The cursor is positioned on the cell you want to name.
PRESS: [Enter]

Figure 4.19

An as-displayed print macro (Lotus 2.2 Learn mode)

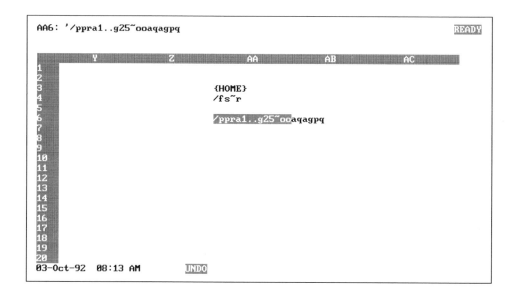

9. Before executing this macro, make sure your printer is on. To execute the print macro, hold down [Alt] and type P. The as-displayed version of the BILLS file should be printing out on your printer.

10. To save your spreadsheet including the as-displayed macro, execute the save macro by holding [Alt] and typing S.

To create a macro that prints BILLS in the cell-formulas format, perform the following steps:

1. To cancel the current Learn range:
TYPE: /
CHOOSE: Worksheet, Learn, Clear

2. Position the cursor in cell AA9, which will mark the beginning of the Learn range.

3. To initiate Menu mode so you can define the Learn range:
    TYPE: /
    CHOOSE: Worksheet, Learn, Range

4. The cursor is positioned at the beginning of the soon-to-be learn range. To anchor the beginning of the Learn range:
    TYPE: .
    To include 20 cells in the Learn range:
    PRESS: [PgDn]
    PRESS: [Enter]
    The spreadsheet should have returned to Ready mode.

5. Now that the Learn range has been defined, it's time to activate the LEARN command and then perform the procedure to print the spreadsheet in the cell-formulas format. As stated previously, it doesn't matter where the cursor is positioned because the keystrokes will automatically record in the Learn range.
    To initiate the LEARN command:
    PRESS: [Alt]+[F5]
    Any key you press will now be recorded in the Learn range—that is, until you turn the LEARN command off. (When choosing commands, remember to type the underlined character of the command option.) Press the following keys to print the spreadsheet in the cell-formulas format:
    TYPE: /
    CHOOSE: Print, Printer, Range
    TYPE: A1..G25
    PRESS: [Enter]
    CHOOSE: Options, Other, Cell-formulas, Quit
    CHOOSE: Align, Go, Page, Quit

6. To turn the LEARN command off:
    PRESS: [Alt]+[F5]

7. When you press one of the cursor-movement keys or [Enter], you'll see the keystrokes in cell AA9 (Figure 4.20).

8. In this step, you will name the keystrokes you have just entered into cell AA9. The cursor should be positioned on cell AA9. To enter Menu mode:
    PRESS: /
    CHOOSE: Range, Name, Create
    Lotus 1-2-3 is now waiting for you to type in a name for the macro.
    TYPE: \c
    PRESS: [Enter]
    The cursor is positioned on the cell you want to name.
    PRESS: [Enter]

Figure 4.20

A cell-formulas
print macro (Lotus
2.2 Learn mode)

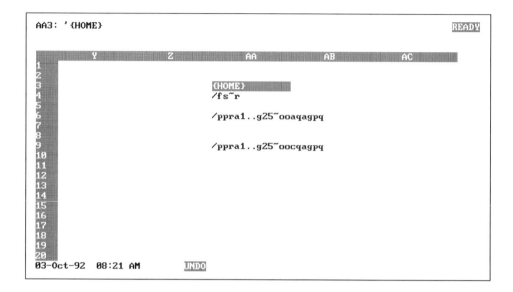

9. Before executing this macro, make sure your printer is on. To execute the print macro, hold **Alt** down and type C.

10. The cell-formulas version of the BILLS file should be printing out on your printer. To save your spreadsheet including the new cell-formulas macro, execute the save macro by holding **Alt** down and typing S.

DOCUMENTING YOUR MACROS

You now have three macros in this spreadsheet. Figure 4.16 shows the three macros in column AA. Column Z lists the names of the macros (for example, S, P, C). After you have created a number of macros, you may forget what you named a particular macro; if you do, look it up in column Z. Column AB provides a brief description of the purpose of each macro.

OTHER USEFUL MACROS

Depending on your spreadsheet application, there are many different macros you may want to include in a given spreadsheet. Following are a few examples:

1. *Consolidation macro.* In this session, you learned how to consolidate data from four quarterly (source) spreadsheets (Q1, Q2, Q3, and Q4) into a target spreadsheet named SUMMARY. As you might have noticed, similar keystrokes were required each time you performed the consolidation

procedure—the only difference was that you moved the cursor to a new target location each time before performing the consolidation procedure. Because of the repetitive nature of the consolidation procedure, it makes sense to automate it using a macro.

2. *Data entry macro.* Often the user is required to move the cursor to certain cells in a spreadsheet and to enter data into them. Macro commands are available that allow users to automate moving the cursor to specified cells. Macros of this type are often referred to as *cursor-movement macros.*

3. *Macro for printing multiple copies of a spreadsheet.* Often more than one copy of a spreadsheet is needed—for example, to distribute to many people at a meeting. In this case, you may want to create a macro to automate printing your spreadsheet a specified number of times.

SUMMARY

In this session you learned how to manage the files you create using a number of different procedures. The WINDOW command, for example, enables you to see two ends or two sides of a very long or very wide spreadsheet. The TITLES command enables you to freeze labels on the screen to serve as a frame of reference as you scroll the screen across or down. The procedure for protecting the cells in your spreadsheets that you don't want to change (such as formulas and descriptive text) is also a very important one. You should use this procedure with every spreadsheet you create so that formulas aren't accidentally erased.

Being able to copy, add, or subtract data from source files into a target file (file consolidation) and to link cells in multiple spreadsheets (file-linking) means that you can work with smaller, more manageable files; in other words, you are in no way restricted to storing all the data that relates to a particular business task (such as keeping track of payroll) in one huge spreadsheet. You can store data in various small spreadsheets and then bring parts of the data into a summary spreadsheet as needed.

In this session, you also learned how to create macros, which can save you time by providing you shortcuts for performing repetitive procedures. Macros enable you to type just two keystrokes to perform a procedure instead of the many keystrokes otherwise required to perform most procedures. Once you become comfortable with using Lotus 1-2-3, you will want to automate your spreadsheet procedures with macros.

COMMAND SUMMARY

The following table provides a list of the commands and procedures covered in this session.

Table 4.1

Command Summary

Name a range of cells	Position the cursor in the first cell of the range to be named, /, Range, Name, Create, type in the range name, (Enter), highlight the range of cells to be named, (Enter)
Use titles (to freeze labels)	Position the cursor to the right of the row headings and/or below the column headings that you want to freeze, /, Worksheet, Titles, choose Both, Horizontal, or Vertical
Clear titles (to unfreeze labels)	/, Worksheet, Titles, Clear
Create a window	Position the cursor to the right of the columns you want on the left side of the window or below the rows you want on the top of the window, /, Worksheet, Window, choose Horizontal or Vertical, use (F6) to move from one window to the other
Clear a window	/, Worksheet, Window, Clear
Use protection	To globally protect the entire spreadsheet: /, Worksheet, Global, Protection, Enable
	To unprotect a range of cells in a spreadsheet: /, Range, Unprotect, highlight the range of cells to be unprotected, (Enter)
Consolidate a spreadsheet range	Position the cursor in the cell you want the data to be consolidated into, /, File, Combine, choose the Add, Subtract, or Copy option, Named/Specified-range, specify the range of cells to be consolidated, highlight the file you want to consolidate data from, (Enter)

Table 4.1 Command Summary (concluded)	Create a macro (without Learn mode)	Perform the procedure manually and write the keystrokes down, type the keystrokes into a cell outside the normal print range, position the cursor on the first cell in the range that contains the keystrokes, /, Range, Name, Create, type a backslash followed by one other character, (Enter)
	Create a macro (with Learn mode)	To define the Learn range: /, Worksheet, Learn, highlight the Learn range, (Enter)
		To create the macro: Press (Alt)+(F5) to initiate the LEARN command, perform the procedure you want to automate, press (Alt)+(F5) to turn the LEARN command off, position the cursor on the first cell in the range that contains the keystrokes, /, Range, Name, Create, type a backslash followed by one other character, (Enter)
	Use a macro	If you named the macro with a backslash and one other character, to execute the, macro, hold (Alt) down and type the "other" character. Otherwise use the RUN command ((Alt)+(F3)) to execute the macro.

KEY TERMS

consolidation procedures   Electronic spreadsheet procedures that enable the user to work with spreadsheets of reaonable size and to copy data from one spreadsheet to another; these procedures make it easier to manage large amounts of spreadsheet data.

file-linking   The ability to put formulas into spreadsheet cells that refer to cells in one or more spreadsheets stored on disk.

LEARN   A Lotus 1-2-3 command that captures your keystrokes so they can be used in a **macro**.

macro   In Lotus 1-2-3, collection of keystrokes that save you time when performing repetitive spreadsheet procedures.

protection procedures   Lotus 1-2-3 procedure used to protect spreadsheet cells from being changed.

range name   In Lotus 1-2-3, a name that has been given to a range of cells.

RANGE NAME CREATE   A Lotus 1-2-3 command that enables you to assign a name to a range of cells.

TITLES   Lotus 1-2-3 command that makes it easier to manage a large spreadsheet by freezing descriptive text (column and row headings) on the screen.

WINDOW   Lotus 1-2-3 command that makes it possible for the user to see both sides or ends of a large spreadsheet on the screen at once.

Window key (F6)   In Lotus 1-2-3, this function key moves the cursor from one window to the other.

EXERCISES

SHORT ANSWER

1. What is the purpose for using protection in a spreadsheet?
2. What does it mean to consolidate data in spreadsheets? Provide an example of when you might want to perform a consolidation procedure.
3. Why are the WINDOW command and the TITLES command used?
4. Describe two ways you can name a macro. How does the way you name a macro affect how you execute the macro?
5. Before consolidating data from another spreadsheet, where should you position the cursor?
6. Before initiating the WINDOW or TITLES command, where should you position the cursor?
7. What steps are required to create a macro using the LEARN command? How does this method for creating a macro differ from creating one without the LEARN command?
8. Describe a few different reasons for using range names in a spreadsheet.
9. You have just typed some macro keystrokes into cell AA5. What must you do before you can use the macro?
10. How can you document your macros? Why is such documentation useful?

HANDS-ON

1. . To practice the consolidation procedure, perform the following steps:
    a. Create the spreadsheet pictured in Figure 4.21 and save it onto your Advantage Diskette as MASTER. (Note: You should use the @SUM function in the range E4..E8 to add the five amounts in columns B, C, and D. Column E will display zeros until you've typed in data.)
    b. Enter data—any numbers that you want—into the MASTER spreadsheet (in the range B4..D8). Save this spreadsheet (with the added data) onto your Advantage Diskette as 1ST.

c. Retrieve a copy of MASTER from the Advantage Diskette. Edit the titles (B2, C2, D2) to reflect the months for quarter two (APR, MAY, JUNE). Change some of the data and save this spreadsheet onto your Advantage Diskette as 2ND.

Figure 4.21

The MASTER spreadsheet

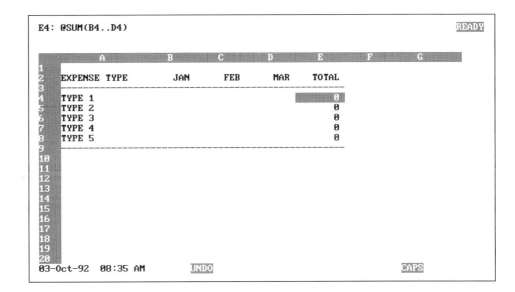

d. Create the spreadsheet pictured in Figure 4.22 (make sure to clear RAM first). (Note: You should use the @SUM function in the range D4..D8 to add the amounts in columns B and C. Column D will display zeros until you've performed the consolidation procedure.) Save this spreadsheet as QUARTERS.

Figure 4.22

The QUARTERS spreadsheet

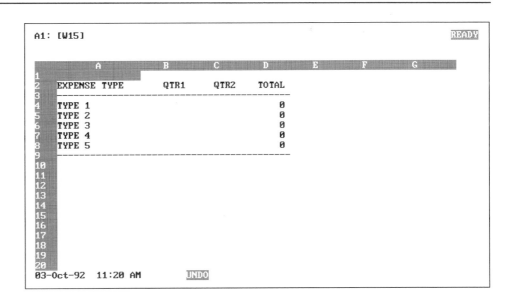

e. Consolidate the range E4..E8 from the 1ST and 2ND spreadsheets into the QUARTERS spreadsheet.

f. Challenge: Create a macro in the QUARTERS spreadsheet that will first erase the range B4..C8, and then consolidate the range E4..E8 from the 1ST and 2ND spreadsheets.

2. To practice using the RANGE NAME command and including range names in formulas:
   a. Retrieve the NAMES spreadsheet from the Advantage Diskette.
   b. Edit all cells that contain the @SUM, @MIN, @MAX, and @AVG functions so that they include range names rather than actual cell references. (You decide what names to use.)
   c. Type your name into cell C1 and then save the spreadsheet onto the Advantage Diskette. Print the spreadsheet in both the as-displayed and cell-formulas formats.

3. To practice creating a save macro and two print macros:
   a. Retrieve NAMES from the Advantage Diskette.
   b. Create a save macro and two print macros (as-displayed and cell-formulas) in this spreadsheet.
   c. Document the macros.
   d. Print a copy of your spreadsheet and your macros.

4. Challenge: Create a spreadsheet that you can use to project your expenses and/or income every six months for the next five years. Make sure to do the following:
   a. Type your name into cell C1.
   b. Use the TITLES command to freeze both the row and column headings on the screen.
   c. Use range names in your formulas. For example, if you add the values in a range of cells, use a range name to refer to the range.
   d. Create a save macro and two print macros (as-displayed and cell-formulas) in this spreadsheet.
   e. Protect all the cells that contain formulas and text. Use the save macro to save the spreadsheet again.
   f. Print the spreadsheet in the As-Displayed format.

5. To practice file-linking, perform the following steps:
   a. Retrieve MARCH from the Advantage Diskette (Figure 4.23).
   b. Include linking formulas in the MARCH spreadsheet that refer to cells in the range G7..G11 in the WEEK1, WEEK2, WEEK3, and WEEK4 files that are stored on the Advantage Diskette. (For example, in cell B7 in the MARCH spreadsheet, include a formula to cell G7 in the WEEK1 spreadsheet.) The WEEK1 file is pictured in Figure 4.24.
   c. Format column G in the percent format to two decimal places. Format the rest of the numbers in this spreadsheet in the currency format to two decimal places.
   d. Include your name in cell C2.

Figure 4.23

The MARCH
spreadsheet

```
A1: 'XYZ COMPANY                                                    READY

       A           B           C           D           E           F
1  XYZ COMPANY              Prepared by:
2  Month:      March        [your name]
3
4  EXPENSE
5  TYPE         WEEK1       WEEK2       WEEK3       WEEK4       TOTAL
6  ----------------------------------------------------------------
7  Paper                                                        0
8  Software                                                     0
9  Disks                                                        0
10 Telephone                                                    0
11 Fed. Express                                                 0
12 ----------------------------------------------------------------
13 TOTAL         0           0           0           0          0
14
15
16 March Expense Tracker
17 --------------------------------------
18 Minimum       0
19 Maximum       0
20 Average       0
03-Oct-92  11:20 AM          UNDO
```

Figure 4.24

The WEEK1
spreadsheet

```
A1: [W13] "XYZ COMPANY                                               READY

       A         B        C        D        E        F        G
1  XYZ COMPANY
2        Week:      1
3
4  EXPENSE
5  TYPE        MON      TUE      WED      THU      FRI     TOTAL
6  -----------------------------------------------------------------
7  Paper         0    69.88       0        0     74.8    144.68
8  Software     19    49.99       0        0    45.99    114.98
9  Disks        56        0      19    99.76        0    174.76
10 Telephone  69.5       54    78.45    56.67   109.45    368.07
11 Fed. Express 22.5    48.6     21.9     111       69     273
12 -----------------------------------------------------------------
13 TOTAL       167   222.47   119.35   267.43   299.24   1075.49
14
15
16
17
18
19
20
03-Oct-92  11:24 AM          UNDO
```

e. Save (and replace) this spreadsheet as MARCH on the Advantage Diskette.

f. Print the spreadsheet in the as-displayed and cell-formulas formats.

SESSION 5

LOTUS 1-2-3:
CREATING GRAPHS

Which would you rather do—squint at a column of numbers to try to see which ones are important, or transform those numbers into a bar or pie chart that will make the important ones stand out graphically? Clearly, the visual method is a quicker way of conveying information. This session shows you how to turn numbers into various kinds of graphics using Lotus 1-2-3.

PREVIEW

When you have completed this session, you will be able to:

Describe the different forms of graphic presentation.
·
Describe the principles of graphic presentation.
·
Create pie charts.
·
Create bar charts.
·
Create line charts.
·
Create a table of graph names.
·
Load Lotus PrintGraph.
·
Use Lotus PrintGraph to print a graph.

SESSION OUTLINE

Why Is This Session Important?

Forms of Business Graphics Presentation

       Pie Charts

       Line Charts

       Bar Charts

       XY Charts

Principles of Graphics Presentation

       Simplicity

       Unity

       Emphasis

       Balance

Saving Graphs: Important Steps to Follow

Using Lotus 1-2-3 to Create and Print Graphs

Creating a Pie Chart

       Exploding and Shading

Creating a Simple Bar Chart

Creating a Stacked-Bar Chart

Creating a Grouped Bar Chart

Creating a Line Chart

Creating a Table of Graph Names

Loading PrintGraph

Printing a Graph

Summary

       Command Summary

Key Terms

Exercises

       Short Answer

       Hands-On

WHY IS THIS SESSION IMPORTANT?

Graphic presentation of data is more effective than using plain text and numbers for the same reason that road maps are easier to follow than written or dictated directions. People seem to remember what they see in the form of images and symbols better than they remember detailed text or speeches. **Graphics,** which are the pictorial representation of words and data, provide us with an effective method of presentation. In this session, you learn how to use Lotus 1-2-3 to graph spreadsheet data.

FORMS OF BUSINESS GRAPHICS PRESENTATION

The most common forms used for presenting business information graphically are (1) pie charts, (2) line charts, (3) bar charts, and (4) XY charts. In the following sections, we refer to the QTR1-EX spreadsheet data shown in Figure 5.1 (you created a spreadsheet like this in Session 2).

Figure 5.1

The QTR1-EX spreadsheet

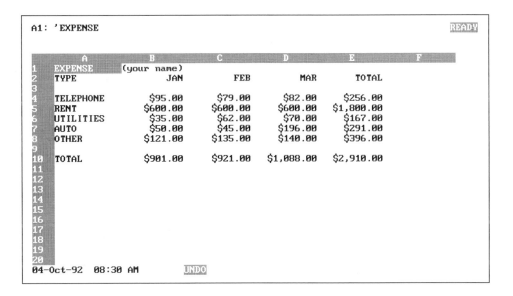

PIE CHARTS

A **pie chart,** which is a circle with wedges that look like slices of pie, is the best chart to use when you are illustrating parts of a whole. For example, you would use a pie chart to show in graphic form what percentage each type of expense in

Figure 5.1 is of the whole (Figure 5.2). To avoid confusion, you should never create a pie chart with more than 12 slices and preferably not more than 8; otherwise, the chart becomes cluttered and loses meaning.

Figure 5.2

Pie chart

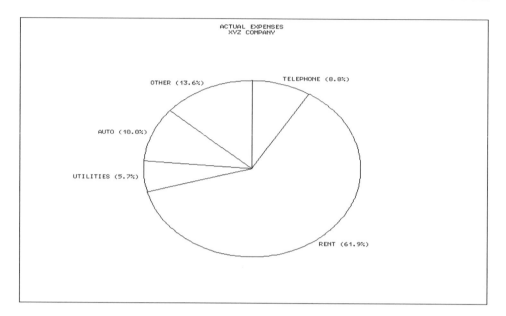

Sometimes the technique of **exploding** is used in pie charts (Figure 5.3). This technique separates a particular part of the chart for emphasis. For example, if you want to emphasize the fact that the OTHER expense category represents a large percentage of TOTAL expenses, you could explode that wedge of the pie chart so that it appears separate from the rest of the wedges.

Figure 5.3

Exploded pie chart. The OTHER pie slice has been separated from the rest of the pie to emphasize that it represents a large percentage of total expenses.

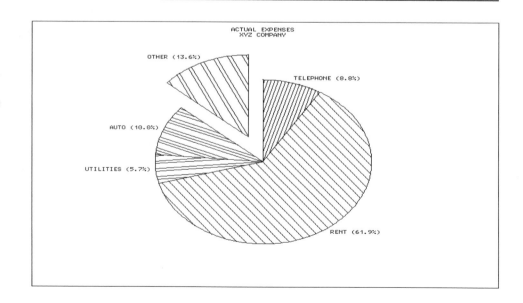

LINE CHARTS

When you need to show trends over time, the **line chart** is the appropriate chart form to use. The angles of the line reflect variations in a trend, and the distance of the line from the horizontal axis represents quantity. For example, if you want to show expense trends over the first three months of the year in the form of a line chart, the chart would look like the one in Figure 5.4.

Figure 5.4

Line chart. Lotus set the Y-scale (that is, the upper and lower limits) automatically.

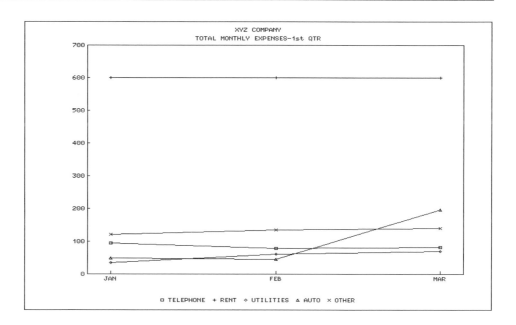

When you create a line chart, you must sometimes define the scale for the vertical axis of the chart by specifying the lowest value (0 in Figure 5.4) and the highest value (700) on the scale, as well as the number of intervals between the two points (6). Usually spreadsheet programs will perform this task for you; however, you may want to adjust the scale yourself. Adjusting the scale can change your perception of a chart. For example, the line chart in Figure 5.4 has an upper limit of 700 with RENT shown along the top. However, the line chart in Figure 5.5 has an upper limit of 200 and the RENT expense isn't graphed because it's off the scale. Note that it's now easier to see that AUTO expenses took a big jump in March and that UTILITIES also increased substantially. If you changed the scale (reduced it) to show RENT, then the increase in AUTO expense would not look so large, although the expense amounts remain the same. In effect, enlarging a scale often makes it easier to understand the data.

Figure 5.5

If you adjust the
Y-scale manually,
the meaning of a
graph can change.

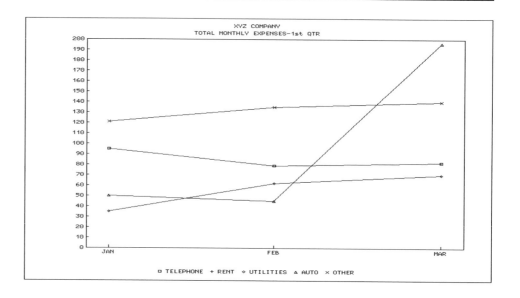

BAR CHARTS

When the purpose is to compare one data element with another data element, a **bar chart** is the appropriate form to use. Figure 5.6 compares the total monthly expense amounts. In this bar chart, it's easy to see that March's expenses were the highest and that January's expenses were the lowest. The chart in Figure 5.6 is a simple bar chart. It provides no information about what types of expenses were incurred. Grouped bar charts and stacked bar charts, variations of the simple bar chart, do give information about types of expenses. A **grouped bar chart** (Figure 5.7) shows how all data elements compare over time. A **stacked bar chart** (Figure 5.8) shows how the components of a data element compare over time.

Figure 5.6

Bar chart

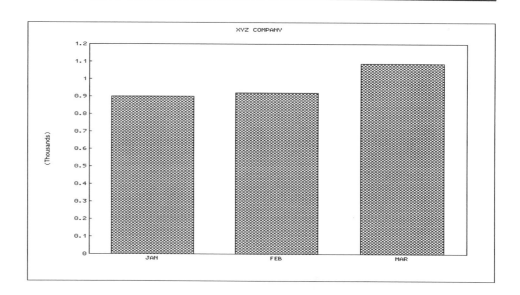

Figure 5.7

Grouped bar
chart

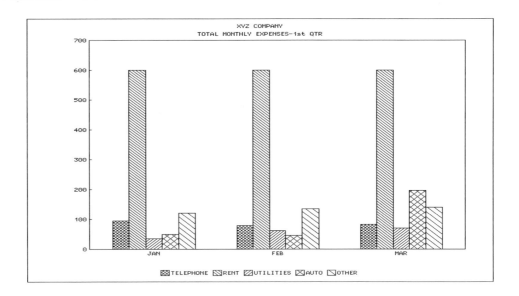

Figure 5.8

Stacked bar
chart

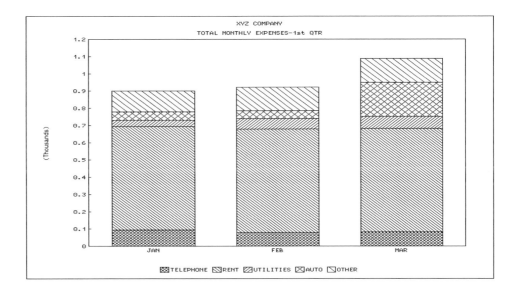

XY CHARTS

XY charts, which are commonly referred to as *scatter charts*, are used to show
how one or more data elements relate to another data element. For example, you
could compare sales and profits (Figure 5.9), tennis court use and average daily
temperature, and so on. Although XY charts look similar to line charts, XY charts
include a numeric scale along the X-axis.

Figure 5.9

XY chart

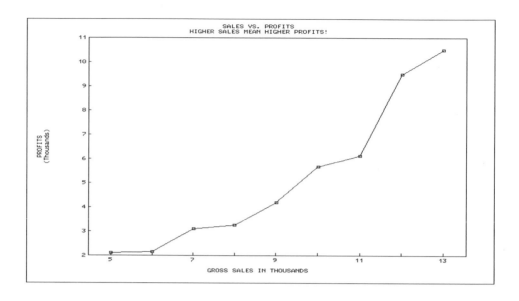

PRINCIPLES OF GRAPHICS PRESENTATION

No matter how sophisticated your graphics software may be, you would probably be better off using no graphics at all if you didn't follow basic principles for creating charts: simplicity, unity, emphasis, and balance. The following sections describe each of these principles.

SIMPLICITY

Many things can cause your chart to look confusing: for example, using too much color, using too much descriptive text, including too many variables (such as too many pie slices in a pie chart). It's natural to try to tell the whole story in one chart, but doing so may defeat the whole purpose of using graphics. You use a chart to symbolize numbers or words because most people tend to find graphics easier to understand than straight text and tables. If you include too much text or detail in a chart, the visual aspects become muddled and the symbols become difficult to understand. Always try to keep your charts simple.

UNITY

To be understandable, your graph must clearly relate all the elements of data it contains—that is, it must appear as a unit. For instance, if you use too much space between the variables (such as between bars in a bar chart), you will probably destroy the unity of your chart. Framing, or boxing, a graph can help to unify it.

EMPHASIS

Emphasis is used to make certain data elements stand out. For example, exploding a pie slice emphasizes that piece of a pie chart. No matter what type of chart you create, you can emphasize different parts using colors and shading.

BALANCE

Your graph should look balanced—both as a unit and in the context of the rest of the page. One factor that affects balance is the position of descriptive text, including titles and legends. Changing the position of such text affects the balance of the graph. Changing the shading, color, and thickness of the lines used in a graph will also affect balance. For instance, if you create a bar chart made up of eight bars, don't specify a dark color for the four larger bars on the right side of the chart and a light color for the smaller bars on the left. Because dark colors appear heavy, they will make the bar chart look out of balance by "weighing down" the right side.

SAVING GRAPHS: IMPORTANT STEPS TO FOLLOW

Lotus provides you with a command that you can use to view a graph as you are creating it. Once you are pleased with how the graph looks on the screen, you should save the graph specifications. *Use the following three steps as part of your save procedure:*

1. *Use the GRAPH SAVE command so you can print your graphs later.*
    To print a graph using Lotus, you must exit Lotus 1-2-3 and load Lotus PrintGraph (the procedure is described later in this session). The GRAPH SAVE command saves your graph specifications in a file that the PrintGraph program can understand. These graph files have the extension PIC.

2. *Use the GRAPH NAME command.*
    This command gives a name to your graph specifications so that you can modify the graph later (you can't modify a graph from within PrintGraph). The output of this command isn't a file; it is simply a name inside the current worksheet that enables you to call up, or reference, the specifications for a particular graph.

3. *Use the FILE SAVE command.*
    This command is used to save any graph names you defined in the preceding step.

USING LOTUS 1-2-3 TO CREATE AND PRINT GRAPHS

No matter what type of graph you are creating, certain steps must be followed to create a graph. Figure 5.10 displays Lotus's graph settings sheet. During the process of creating a graph, you will fill in this settings sheet with your graph specifications. Once you have created a graph, you will probably want to print it. The rest of this session describes in detail the steps for creating and printing graphs.

Figure 5.10

Lotus's graph settings sheet

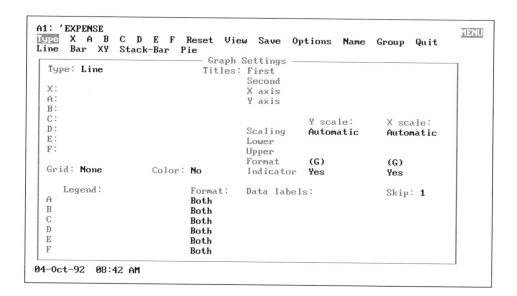

The following is an overview of the process:

1. Call up the Graph settings sheet.

2. Clear any graph specifications from RAM that may have been left over from a previously created graph.

3. Select the graph type.

4. Select the data ranges to be graphed. Lotus lets you define up to six data ranges (A, B, C, D, E, and F). For example, Figure 5.11 labels the data ranges in a spreadsheet and displays a bar graph of the data.

Figure 5.11(a)

Graph ranges are
displayed in the
spreadsheet.

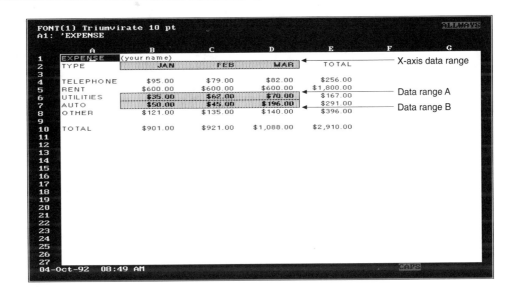

Figure 5.11(b)

The graph ranges
in Figure 5.11(a)
are displayed in a
graph. In addition,
the components
of a typical graph
have been labelled.

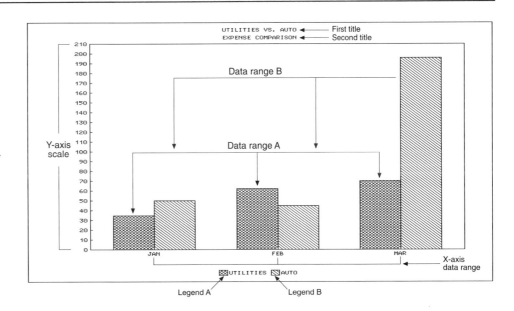

5. Add data labels (if applicable). (A *data label*—usually a number—identifies, for example, each point on a line chart, or the value of each bar in a bar chart.)

6. Add titles and legends (if applicable), or use one or more of the other graph options available (Table 5.1) (A *legend* is descriptive text, usually a word, that identifies each data range.)

Table 5.1	Legend	Used to label the A–F data ranges.
Graph Options	Format	In line and XY graphs, this option enables you to choose whether data points are connected with lines, symbols, lines and symbols, or neither lines nor symbols.
	Titles	Used to add first and second titles, and X-axis and Y-axis titles.
	Grid	Adds or removes horizontal or vertical grid lines in a graph.
	Scale	Determines axis scaling and the format of the numbers on the axis.
	Color	If you are using a color monitor, this option enables you to display your graphs in color.
	B&W	Causes Lotus 1-2-3 to display graphs in black and white.
	Data-Labels	Uses the cell contents of a data range as labels for the bars or points in a graph.
	Quit	Exits you to the Graph menu.

7. Name the graph.

8. Save the graph.

9. Save the spreadsheet. Then exit Lotus 1-2-3 and load PrintGraph.

10. Choose the graph(s) you want to print.

Before proceeding, make sure the following are true:

1. You have loaded Lotus 1-2-3 and are displaying an empty spreadsheet template on the screen.

2. Your Advantage Diskette is inserted in the drive. You will save your work onto the diskette and retrieve the files that have been created for you. (Note: The Advantage Diskette can be made by copying all the files off the instructor's Master Advantage Diskette onto a formatted diskette.)

CREATING A PIE CHART

In this section you will create a pie chart that shows what percentage each type of expense is of total expenses. When you are done, the pie chart should look similar to the one pictured in Figure 5.2. Perform the following steps to create the pie chart:

1. Retrieve QTR1-EX from the Advantage Diskette (the procedure for retrieving is described in Session 2).

2. To initiate the GRAPH command:
    TYPE: /
    CHOOSE: Graph

3. A list of graph options should be displaying on top of the screen (Figure 5.12). To specify the type of graph you want to create:
    CHOOSE: Type, Pie

4. Now you need to define where the data to be graphed is stored, which involves identifying the A data range. *Note: Since this chart is only graphing one data range, you need to only specify an A range. If the chart involved more than one data range, you would first identify the A range, and then the B range, C range, and so on.* The data you want to graph is stored in the range of cells E4..E8.
    CHOOSE: A
    TYPE: E4..E8
    PRESS: Enter
    E4..E8 is now listed on the left side of the Graph settings sheet next to A:.

Figure 5.12

The Graph menu. The cursor is currently highlighting the Type option.

```
A1: 'EXPENSE                                                           MENU
Type  X  A  B  C  D  E  F  Reset  View  Save  Options  Name  Group  Quit
Line  Bar  XY  Stack-Bar  Pie
                              ───── Graph Settings ─────
  Type: Line                  Titles: First
                                      Second
  X:                                  X axis
  A:                                  Y axis
  B:
  C:                                            Y scale:      X scale:
  D:                                  Scaling   Automatic     Automatic
  E:                                  Lower
  F:                                  Upper
                                      Format    (G)           (G)
  Grid: None        Color: No         Indicator Yes           Yes

    Legend:                 Format:   Data labels:            Skip: 1
  A                         Both
  B                         Both
  C                         Both
  D                         Both
  E                         Both
  F                         Both


04-Oct-92  08:57 AM                                              CAPS
```

5. To see what your graph looks like at this point, choose the View option:
    CHOOSE: View
    Your pie chart should be displaying on the screen (Figure 5.13). In the next few steps you will define the title for your chart and the descriptive text for each piece of the pie. *Note: When Lotus 1-2-3 is in Ready mode, you can view the current graph specifications by pressing* F10.

Figure 5.13

Creating a pie chart. The A data range (E4..E8) has been defined.

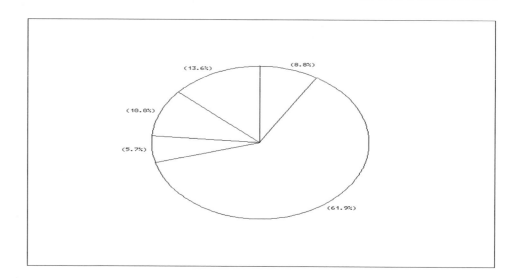

PRESS: *any key to display the Graph settings menu*

....

Quick Reference

Viewing a Graph

Two methods are available for viewing the current graph specifications. First, from within the main Graph menu, you can choose the View option or, second, press F10 when Lotus is in Ready mode.

....

7. To define the title for the graph, you must first choose the OPTIONS command and then the Titles option.
    CHOOSE: Options
    Note: When displaying the Graph Settings menu, you can use F6 *(Window) at any time to view the spreadsheet.*
    To create the main, or "first," title:
    CHOOSE: Titles, First
    TYPE: ACTUAL EXPENSES
    PRESS: Enter

8. To create the subtitle, or "second" title:
    CHOOSE: Titles, Second
    TYPE: XYZ COMPANY
    PRESS: (Enter)

9. Specifying the descriptive text that will identify the different pieces of the pie involves choosing the X option. To move up in the menu hierarchy so you can access the X option:
    PRESS: (Esc)

10. To choose the X option and then specify the range A4..A8:
    CHOOSE: X
    TYPE: A4..A8
    PRESS: (Enter)

11. To view the completed graph on the screen:
    CHOOSE: View
    The graph should look similar to Figure 5.2.

12. To display the Graph menu:
    PRESS: *any key*

To give a name to the specifications for this pie chart so that you can view this chart at a later date, perform the following steps:

1. CHOOSE: Name, Create

2. To name the specifications PIE1:
    TYPE: PIE1
    PRESS: (Enter)

The next step uses the GRAPH SAVE command to save the chart into a format that PrintGraph can understand so that you can print the graph. When you do this, Lotus will create a file on your disk that has the extension of PIC.

1. The Graph settings menu should be displaying on the screen.
    CHOOSE: Save

2. To save the graph onto your Advantage Diskette as PIE1.PIC (the PIC extension will automatically be supplied):
    TYPE: PIE1
    PRESS: (Enter)

3. To exit the Graph menu and return to menu mode:
    CHOOSE: Quit

Quick Reference

Naming and Saving a Graph

1. Within the Graph settings menu:
    CHOOSE: Name, Create
2. TYPE: *a name for the graph*
    PRESS: [Enter]
3. To save the graph in the form of a graph file that has the extension of PIC:
    CHOOSE: Save
4. TYPE: *a filename for the graph*
    PRESS: [Enter]

To save the QTR1-EX spreadsheet with the named PIE1 specifications:

1. Initiate Menu mode (/).

2. CHOOSE: File, Save

3. To save the file onto the same disk using the same name (QTR1-EX):
    PRESS: [Enter]

4. To replace the copy on disk with the contents of RAM:
    CHOOSE: Replace

EXPLODING AND SHADING

To include an exploded pie piece or shading in a graph (Figure 5.3), you must specify a B range that is composed of values with specific characteristics (Figure 5.14; column F). The numbers in the B range must be numbered consecutively beginning with either 0 or 1. If you don't want the chart to include shading, the values in the B range must begin with the number 0 (0, 1, 2, and so on). If you do want shading, the values in the B range must begin with the number 1 (1, 2, 3, and so on). Each number corresponds directly to a different cell in the A range. If you add 100 to a number in the B range, the corresponding pie slice will appear exploded, or separate, from the rest of the pie slices.

In this step you will modify the QTR1-EX spreadsheet to include a B range and define the B range in the Graph menu. You will then save the graph specifications.

1. Position the cursor in the following cells and type in the corresponding numbers:

Move to Cell	TYPE:
F4	1
F5	2
F6	3
F7	4
F8	105

Figure 5.14

Creating an exploded pie chart. The range F4..F8 will be defined as the B data range. Because the OTHER data corresponds directly to the value in the B range that has 100 added to it, the OTHER pie slice will appear exploded.

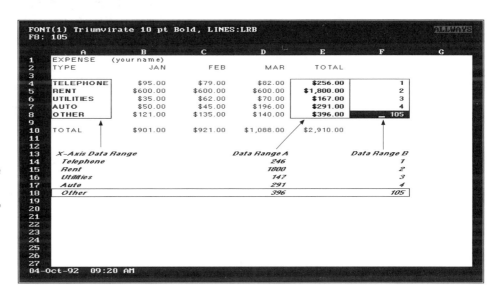

2. To define the B range as the range F4..F8, first initiate menu mode and then choose the Graph option:
    TYPE: /
    CHOOSE: Graph

3. To choose the B option and then specify the range F4..F8:
    CHOOSE: B
    TYPE: F4..F8
    PRESS: Enter

4. To view the graph:
    CHOOSE: View
    The chart should look similar to Figure 5.3; shading is included in this graph because the B range began with the number 1.

5. Press any key to display the Graph menu.

You must specify a B range that has certain characteristics.
a. If the values in the B range are numbered consecutively beginning with zero (0, 1, 2, and so on), the graph won't include shading.
b. If the values in the B range are numbered consecutively beginning with 1 (1, 2, 3, and so on), the graph will include shading.
c. To explode a pie piece, add 100 to a value in the B range.

To give a name to the specifications for this exploded pie chart so that you can view this chart at a later date, perform the following steps:

1. The Graph settings menu should be displaying on the screen.

2. CHOOSE: Name, Create
   TYPE: EXPLODED
   PRESS: (Enter)

Save the specifications for the pie chart into a file that PrintGraph can understand (a PIC file):

1. The Graph menu should be displaying on the screen.
   CHOOSE: Save
   TYPE: EXPLODED
   PRESS: (Enter)

2. To exit the Graph menu and return to Ready mode:
   CHOOSE: Quit

To save the QTR1-EX spreadsheet with the named EXPLODED specifications:

1. To save the QTR1-EX spreadsheet:
   TYPE: /
   CHOOSE: File, Save

2. To save the file onto the same disk using the same name (QTR1-EX):
   PRESS: (Enter)

3. To replace the copy on disk with the contents of RAM:
   CHOOSE: Replace

CREATING A SIMPLE BAR CHART

In this section you will use the QTR1-EX spreadsheet to create a bar chart that compares XYZ Company's monthly expense totals. When you are done, the bar chart should look similar to the one in Figure 5.6.

The bar chart you create here will include the same first and second titles as the pie chart you created in the last section. The data you are graphing is in the range B10..D10, and the X-axis labels are in the range B2..D2. Perform the following steps to create this chart, name it, save the graph specifications, and then save the QTR1-EX file. Before you begin, however, you will clear from RAM the graph specifications of the previous graph (the exploded pie chart) you created.

To clear RAM of the previous graph specifications and prepare to set new ones:

1. TYPE: /
   CHOOSE: Graph, Reset

2. To reset the specifications for the entire graph:
   CHOOSE: Graph

....

Quick Reference   1.   Initiate Menu mode (/).
Clearing Graph   2.   Choose: Graph, Reset, Graph
Specifications

....

Perform the following steps to specify the characteristics for the bar chart:

1. The Graph settings menu should be displaying on the screen. To specify the type of graph you want to create:
   CHOOSE: Type, Bar

2. Now you need to define where the data to be graphed is stored, which involves identifying the A data range. The data you want to graph is stored in the range of cells B10..D10.
   CHOOSE: A
   TYPE: B10..D10
   PRESS: (Enter)

3. To see what your graph looks like at this point:
   CHOOSE: View
   Your bar chart should be displaying on the screen (Figure 5.15).

Figure 5.15

Creating a bar
chart. The A data
range (B10..D10)
has been defined.

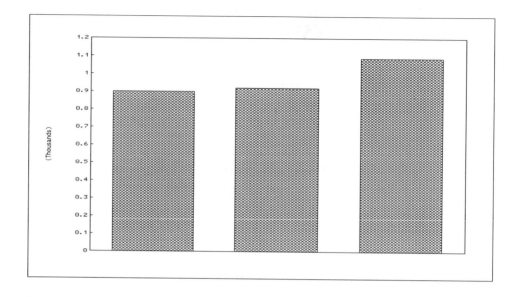

PRESS: *any key to display the Graph settings menu*

4. In this step you need to identify another range. Specifically, you need to define
    the labels for the X-axis (the horizontal axis) by choosing the X option. The
    labels for the X-axis are stored in the range B2..D2.
    CHOOSE: X
    TYPE: B2..D2
    PRESS: (Enter)

5. And finally, to create the main, or "first," title:
    CHOOSE: Options, Titles, First
    TYPE: ACTUAL EXPENSES
    PRESS: (Enter)

6. To create the subtitle, or "second" title:
    CHOOSE: Titles, Second
    TYPE: XYZ COMPANY
    PRESS: (Enter)

7. To view the completed graph on the screen, you must first move up the menu
    hierarchy one level.
    PRESS: (Esc)
    CHOOSE: View
    The screen should look like Figure 5.6.

8. Press any key to display the Graph settings menu.

To name the graph specifications:

1. The graph menu should be displaying on the screen.

2. CHOOSE: Name, Create
   TYPE: BAR1
   PRESS: [Enter]

To save the graph specifications into a file that PrintGraph can understand:

1. The graph menu should be displaying on the screen.
   CHOOSE: Save
   TYPE: BAR1
   PRESS: [Enter]

2. To exit the Graph menu and return to Ready mode:
   CHOOSE: Quit

To save the QTR1-EX spreadsheet with the named bar chart specifications:

1. To save the QTR1-EX spreadsheet:
   TYPE: /
   CHOOSE: File, Save

2. To save the file onto the same disk using the same name (QTR1-EX):
   PRESS: [Enter]

3. To replace the copy on disk with the contents of RAM:
   CHOOSE: Replace

CREATING A STACKED BAR CHART

In this section you will create a stacked bar chart that compares XYZ Company's monthly expense totals. This chart is similar to the bar chart you created in the last section; however, this chart will provide information about what expenses make up each bar. You will need to identify five data ranges in this chart (A, B, C, D, and E). When you are done, the bar chart should look similar to the one in Figure 5.8.

First, to clear RAM of the previous graph specifications and prepare to set new specifications:

To enter Menu mode and then choose the Graph option:
TYPE: /
CHOOSE: Graph, Reset, Graph

Perform the following steps to specify the characteristics for the stacked bar chart:

1. To tell Lotus 1-2-3 what type of graph you want to create:
    CHOOSE: Type, Stack-Bar

2. Now you need to define where the data to be graphed is stored, which involves identifying a few different data ranges. The data for the A range (Telephone) is stored in the range of cells B4..D4.
    CHOOSE: A
    TYPE: B4..D4
    PRESS: [Enter]

3. The data for the B range (Rent) is stored in the range of cells B5..D5.
    CHOOSE: B
    TYPE: B5..D5
    PRESS: [Enter]

4. The data for the C range (Utilities) is stored in the range of cells B6..D6.
    CHOOSE: C
    TYPE: B6..D6
    PRESS: [Enter]

5. The data for the D range (Auto) is stored in the range of cells B7..D7.
    CHOOSE: D
    TYPE: B7..D7
    PRESS: [Enter]

6. The data for the E range (Other) is stored in the range of cells B8..D8.
    CHOOSE: E
    TYPE: B8..D8
    PRESS: [Enter]

7. To see what your graph looks like at this point:
    CHOOSE: View
    The stacked bar chart should be displaying on the screen (Figure 5.16).
    PRESS: *any key to display the Graph settings menu*

In the next few steps, you will define the labels for the X-axis and then the titles for the graph:

1. To choose the X option and then specify the range B2..D2:
    CHOOSE: X
    TYPE: B2..D2
    PRESS: [Enter]

Figure 5.16

Creating a stacked
bar chart. Five data
ranges have been
defined.

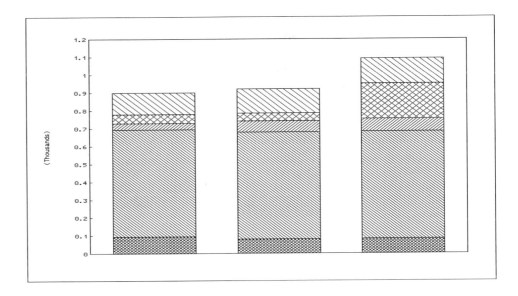

2. To define the title for the graph:
   TYPE: Options
   To create the main, or "first," title:
   CHOOSE: Titles, First
   TYPE: XYZ COMPANY
   PRESS: Enter

3. To create the subtitle, or "second" title:
   CHOOSE: Titles, Second
   TYPE: TOTAL MONTHLY EXPENSES—1st QTR
   PRESS: Enter

4. To see what your graph looks like at this point, first press Esc (to move up
   one level in the Graph menu) and then choose the View option:
   PRESS: Esc
   CHOOSE: View
   The stacked bar chart with added titles should be displaying on the screen.
   PRESS: *any key to display the Graph menu*

To identify what each bar represents you need to define the legend for each bar.
To accomplish this, perform the following steps:

1. CHOOSE: Options

2. To choose the Legend option and then create a legend for the A range:
   CHOOSE: Legend, A
   TYPE: TELEPHONE
   PRESS: Enter

3. To choose the Legend option and then create a legend for the B range:
   CHOOSE: Legend, B
   TYPE: RENT
   PRESS: (Enter)

4. To choose the Legend option and then create a legend for the C range:
   CHOOSE: Legend, C
   TYPE: UTILITIES
   PRESS: (Enter)

5. To choose the Legend option and then create a legend for the D range:
   CHOOSE: Legend, D
   TYPE: AUTO
   PRESS: (Enter)

6. To choose the Legend option and then create a legend for the E range:
   CHOOSE: Legend, E
   TYPE: OTHER
   PRESS: (Enter)
   The screen (displaying all the current graph settings) should look like Figure 5.17.

Figure 5.17

Graph settings. The Graph settings sheet allows you to view all the current graph settings on the screen at once.

```
F8: 105
                                                                    MENU
Legend  Format  Titles  Grid  Scale  Color  B&W  Data-Labels  Quit
Create legends for data ranges
                              ┌──────── Graph Settings ────────
   Type: Stack-Bar            Titles: First  XYZ COMPANY
                                      Second TOTAL MONTHLY EXPENSES-1st QTR
   X: B2..D2                          X axis
   A: B4..E4                          Y axis
   B: B5..D5
   C: B6..D6                                  Y scale:      X scale:
   D: B7..D7                          Scaling  Automatic     Automatic
   E: B8..D8                          Lower
   F:                                 Upper
                                      Format    (G)           (G)
   Grid: None       Color: No         Indicator Yes           Yes

      Legend:              Format:    Data labels:            Skip: 1
   A  TELEPHONE            Both
   B  RENT                 Both
   C  UTILITIES            Both
   D  AUTO                 Both
   E  OTHER                Both
   F                       Both

04-Oct-92   09:46 AM                                            CAPS
```

7. To see what your graph looks like at this point, first press (Esc) (to move up one level in the graph menu) and then choose the View option:
   PRESS: (Esc)
   CHOOSE: View
   The stacked bar chart should be displaying on the screen (Figure 5.8).
   PRESS: *any key to display the Graph settings menu*

To name the graph specifications:

1. The Graph menu should be displaying on the screen.

2. CHOOSE: Name, Create
    TYPE: BAR2
    PRESS: [Enter]

To save the graph specifications into a file that PrintGraph can understand:

1. The graph menu should be displaying on the screen.

2. CHOOSE: Save
    TYPE: BAR2
    PRESS: [Enter]

3. To exit the Graph menu and return to Ready mode:
    CHOOSE: Quit

Save the QTR1-EX spreadsheet with the named stacked bar chart specifications:

1. To save the QTR1-EX spreadsheet:
    TYPE: /
    CHOOSE: File, Save

2. To save the file onto the same disk using the same name (QTR1-EX):
    PRESS: [Enter]

3. To replace the copy on disk with the contents of RAM:
    CHOOSE: Replace

CREATING A GROUPED BAR CHART

In this section you will create a grouped bar chart that compares XYZ Company's monthly expense totals. This chart is similar to the stacked bar chart you created in the last section; however, this chart compares the expenses individually over January, February, and March. Because the charts are so similar, you will use the graph specifications you created in the last section, except change the "type" from stacked bar to bar. When you are done, the bar chart should look similar to the one pictured in Figure 5.7.

To tell Lotus 1-2-3 you want to use the BAR2 specifications:

1. Enter Menu mode and then choose the Graph option:
   TYPE: /
   CHOOSE: Graph

2. Specify that you want to use the BAR2 specifications:
   CHOOSE: Name, Use
   TYPE: BAR2
   PRESS: Enter
   The stacked bar chart should be displaying on the screen.
   PRESS: *any key to display the Graph settings menu*

The type of chart you are creating in this section is bar. Perform the following steps to create this chart:

1. The Graph menu should be displaying on the screen. To change the type of chart:
   CHOOSE: Type, Bar

2. To view the completed chart:
   CHOOSE: View
   The grouped bar chart should look similar to Figure 5.7.

3. PRESS: *any key to display the Graph settings menu*

To name the graph specifications:

1. The Graph settings menu should be displaying on the screen.

2. CHOOSE: Name, Create
   TYPE: BAR3
   PRESS: Enter

To save the graph specifications into a file that PrintGraph can understand:

1. The Graph menu should be displaying on the screen.

2. CHOOSE: Save
   TYPE: BAR3
   PRESS: Enter

3. To exit the Graph menu and return to Ready mode:
   CHOOSE: Quit

Save the QTR1-EX spreadsheet with the named grouped bar chart specifications:

1. To save the QTR1-EX spreadsheet:
    TYPE: /
    CHOOSE: File, Save

2. To save the file onto the same disk using the same name (QTR1-EX):
    PRESS: [Enter]

3. To replace the copy on disk with the contents of RAM:
    CHOOSE: Replace

CREATING A LINE CHART

In this section you create a line chart that compares XYZ Company's monthly expense totals over time. When you are done, the line chart should look similar to Figure 5.4. To create this chart, all you have to do is change the type of the BAR3 chart you created earlier from bar to line. All the other graph specifications are already correct (such as titles and legends).

Do the following to tell Lotus 1-2-3 you want to use the BAR3 specifications:

1. To enter Menu mode and then choose the Graph option:
    TYPE: /
    CHOOSE: Graph

2. To specify that you want to use the BAR3 specifications:
    CHOOSE: Name, Use
    TYPE: BAR3
    PRESS: [Enter]
    The grouped bar chart should be displaying on the screen.
    PRESS: *any key to display the Graph settings menu*

Perform the following steps to create the line chart:

1. The Graph menu should be displaying on the screen. To create a line chart:
    CHOOSE: Type, Line

2. To view the completed chart:
    CHOOSE: View
    The line chart should be displaying on the screen (Figure 5.4).

3. PRESS: *any key to display the Graph settings menu*

To name the graph specifications:

1. The Graph settings menu should be displaying on the screen.

2. CHOOSE: Name, Create
    TYPE: LINE1
    PRESS: [Enter]

To save the graph specifications into a file that PrintGraph can understand:

1. The Graph menu should be displaying on the screen. To choose the Save option:
    CHOOSE: Save

2. To save the graph onto your data disk as LINE1.PIC:
    TYPE: LINE1
    PRESS: [Enter]

3. To exit the Graph menu and return to Ready mode:
    CHOOSE: Quit

Save the QTR1-EX spreadsheet with the named line chart specifications:

1. To save the QTR1-EX spreadsheet:
    TYPE: /
    CHOOSE: File, Save

2. To save the file onto the same disk using the same name (QTR1-EX):
    PRESS: [Enter]

3. To replace the copy on disk with the contents of RAM:
    CHOOSE: Replace

CREATING A TABLE OF GRAPH NAMES

To generate a list of the graph names you have defined, you can use the GRAPH NAME TABLE command. The list of names is placed where the cursor is positioned, so make sure the cursor is in an unused section of your spreadsheet report.

Perform the following steps to generate a list of graph names in cell B13:

1. Initiate Menu mode.
    TYPE: /

2. CHOOSE: Graph, Name, Table

3. Position the cursor in cell B14.

4. With the cursor positioned in cell B14:
    PRESS: Enter
    CHOOSE: Quit
    The screen should look like Figure 5.18.

Figure 5.18

A table of graph names. The first column identifies the name of the chart. The second column identifies the type of chart you created. The third column displays the first title.

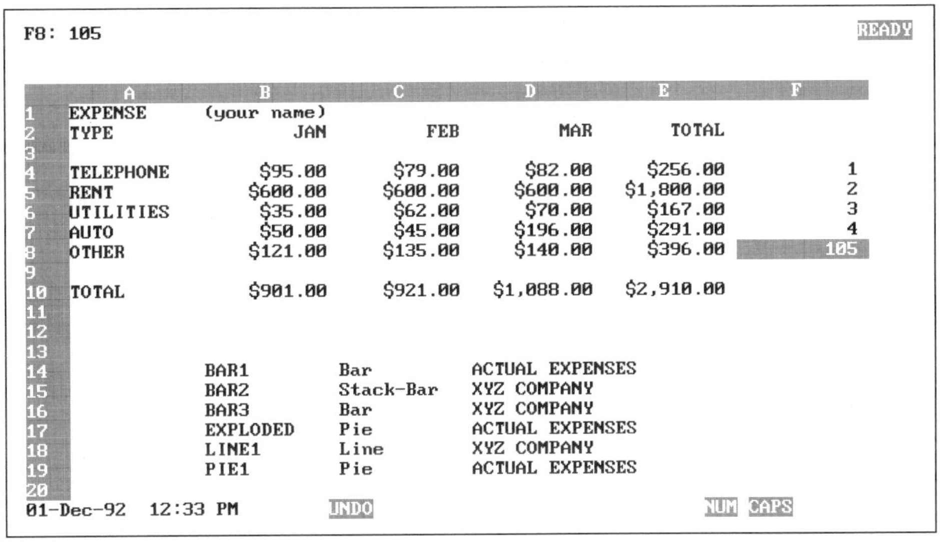

```
F8: 105                                                               READY

         A           B           C           D           E           F
1  EXPENSE     (your name)
2  TYPE                JAN         FEB         MAR        TOTAL
3
4  TELEPHONE       $95.00      $79.00      $82.00      $256.00          1
5  RENT           $600.00     $600.00     $600.00    $1,800.00          2
6  UTILITIES       $35.00      $62.00      $70.00      $167.00          3
7  AUTO            $50.00      $45.00     $196.00      $291.00          4
8  OTHER          $121.00     $135.00     $140.00      $396.00        105
9
10 TOTAL          $901.00     $921.00   $1,088.00    $2,910.00
11
12
13
14             BAR1        Bar         ACTUAL EXPENSES
15             BAR2        Stack-Bar   XYZ COMPANY
16             BAR3        Bar         XYZ COMPANY
17             EXPLODED    Pie         ACTUAL EXPENSES
18             LINE1       Line        XYZ COMPANY
19             PIE1        Pie         ACTUAL EXPENSES
20
01-Dec-92  12:33 PM        UNDO                            NUM CAPS
```

Quick Reference

Creating a Table of Graph Names

1. Initiate Menu mode.
2. CHOOSE: Graph, Name, Table
3. Position the cursor where you want the table (list) to appear, and then press Enter.
4. CHOOSE: Quit

LOADING PRINTGRAPH

To load PrintGraph, you must exit Lotus 1-2-3 so that the Lotus Access System is displaying on the screen; then choose the PrintGraph option. If you are using a diskette system, once you choose the PrintGraph option from the Lotus Access System menu, you will be prompted to insert the PrintGraph diskette.

Perform the following steps to first save the QTR1-EX spreadsheet and then load and use the PrintGraph program:

1. To save the QTR1-EX spreadsheet:
    TYPE: /
    CHOOSE: File, Save
    PRESS: (Enter)
    CHOOSE: Replace

2. To exit Lotus 1-2-3 and display the Lotus Access System menu:
    TYPE: /
    CHOOSE: Quit, Yes
    The Lotus Access System should be displaying on the screen. *Note: If the system prompt (C:\>) is displaying on your screen instead of the Lotus Access System, type PGRAPH and then press (Enter) to load PrintGraph. (If this procedure successfully loads PrintGraph, skip the next step.) If you still have a problem loading PrintGraph, ask your instructor or lab assistant.*

3. To choose the PrintGraph option:
    CHOOSE: PrintGraph
    The screen should look similar to Figure 5.19.

Figure 5.19

The PrintGraph
opening screen

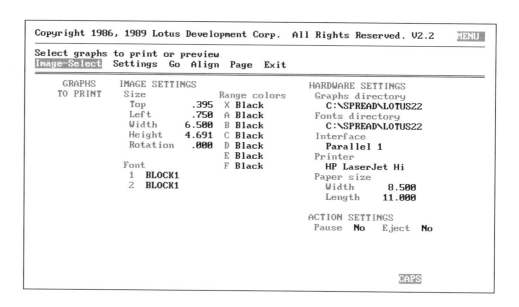

The screen displays the current PrintGraph assumptions—you can change any of these using the SETTINGS command. For example, PrintGraph assumes your graphs will print in a certain size. In addition, PrintGraph assumes you will retrieve your graph files from a certain disk as indicated below the text "Graphs directory."

If the screen isn't displaying A: below the text "Graphs directory," follow the steps below:

1. CHOOSE: Settings, Hardware, Graphs-Directory

2. To tell PrintGraph that your Advantage Diskette is in drive A:
   TYPE: A:
   PRESS: Enter

3. To display the main PrintGraph menu:
   CHOOSE: Quit, Quit

PrintGraph now knows where your graph files are stored.

PRINTING A GRAPH

To print a graph you must exit Lotus 1-2-3 and then load PrintGraph from the Lotus Access System (you did this in the last section). Once PrintGraph has been loaded, you'll use the steps summarized here and detailed in the next list.

1. Make sure PrintGraph knows where the diskette that contains your graph files is located.

2. Choose a graph to print. To select an image, highlight the image and then press the Space Bar to choose the image. By pressing the Space Bar, you place a pound sign (#) next to the filename. If after pressing the Space Bar you decide you don't want to print the graph, press the Space Bar again, and the # will disappear.

To print a graph, perform the following steps:

1. The main PrintGraph menu should be displaying on the screen.
   CHOOSE: Image-Select
   The screen should look like Figure 5.20.

2. To choose one or more graphs to print, highlight the graph(s) and then press the Space Bar.

3. To view a marked graph, press F10. Then press the Space Bar to again view the list of graph files. *(Note: If the message "Fonts directory does not exist" displays, you must specify the correct directory using the SETTINGS HARDWARE command. If you don't know the name of the fonts directory, ask your instructor or lab assistant.)*

Figure 5.20

This list of .PIC files appears after you choose the Image-Select option. To choose a picture to print, highlight the picture and then press the Space Bar.

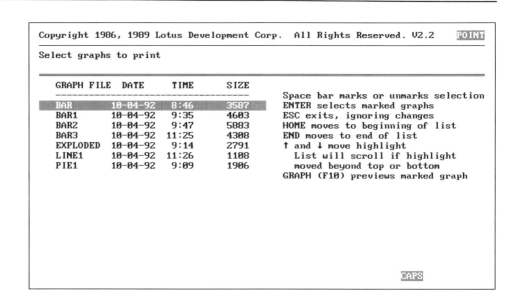

4. To select the marked pictures, press (Enter). The main PrintGraph menu should be displaying on the screen.

5. To print a marked graph:
    CHOOSE: Align, Go

When you are finished using PrintGraph, you will want to exit to the Lotus Access System. Perform the following steps:

CHOOSE: Exit, Yes

The Lotus Access System should again be displaying on the screen.

SUMMARY

When spreadsheet data is presented in graphical form, for example, in a pie chart or bar chart, it is often easier to gain understanding from the data and to form conclusions. Lotus 1-2-3 enables you to display data in graphical form using the following business charts: line, bar, XY, stack-bar, and pie.

As you create a chart, you can view the current graph specifications on the Graph settings sheet. For example, you can see what cells you used in each data range. After you create a chart it is important to give a name to the graph specifications using the GRAPH NAME command so you can view and edit the graph specifications later. If you want to print the graph, use the GRAPH SAVE command, which creates a file that Lotus PrintGraph can understand. And finally, make sure to save your spreadsheet using the FILE SAVE command so that the named graph specifications are saved for later viewing.

COMMAND SUMMARY

The following table provides a list of the commands and procedures covered in this session.

Table 5.2

Command Summary

Exploding and Shading a Pie Segment	Include a B range and remember the following: (a) if the values in the B range are number consecutively beginning with zero, the graph won't include shading, (b) if the values in the B range are numbered consecutively beginning with 1, the graph will include shading, and (c) to explode a pie piece, add 100 to a value in the B range.
Naming and saving graph specifications	/, Graph, Name, Create, type in a name for the graph, (Enter), Save, type a filename in for the graph, (Enter)
Viewing a graph	/, Graph, View, or Press (F10) when Lotus is in Ready mode
Clearing graph specifications	/, Graph, Reset, Graph
Creating a table of graph names	/, Graph, Name, Table, position the cursor where you want the table (list) to appear, (Enter), Quit

---

KEY TERMS

bar chart   This chart, which is made up of bars of varying lengths, compares one data element with another data element.

exploding   The process of separating one piece of a **pie chart** from the rest of the chart.

graphics   The pictorial presentation of words and data.

grouped bar chart   Variation of the **simple bar chart**; shows how all data elements compare over time.

line chart   Shows trends over time; the angles of the line reflect variations in a trend, and the distance of the line from the horizontal axis represents quantity.

pie chart   Circle with wedges that look like pie slices; best chart to use when illustrating parts of a whole.

stacked bar chart   Variation of the simple bar chart; shows how the components of a data element compare over time.

XY chart   Charts used to show how one or more data elements relate to another data element.

EXERCISES

SHORT ANSWER

1. Why is it important to name the graph specifications before saving your spreadsheet?
2. Describe the basic principles of graphic presentation.
3. What is the purpose of saving your graph specifications in the form of a graphics file that has the extension of PIC?
4. What basic steps must you follow to create a graph?
5. Why is the GRAPH NAME TABLE command useful?
6. What do you have to do if you want to shade the segments in a pie chart?
7. What are XY charts typically used for?
8. When saving a graph, what three steps should you follow?
9. Describe the procedure for using PrintGraph.
10. What do you have to do if you want to explode a pie chart segment?

HANDS-ON

1. Using a spreadsheet on the Advantage Diskette called WEEKLY (Figure 5.21), create the following charts:

Figure 5.21

The WEEKLY spreadsheet

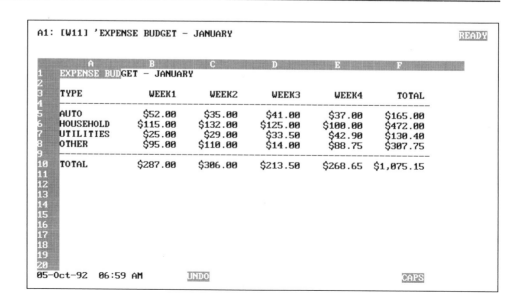

a. Create a bar chart to compare January's weekly expense totals. The data you will graph is in the range B10..E10. Include X-axis labels. Also include the following titles and then name and save the graph as BAR-EX1A.
First Title: EXPENSE BUDGET
Second Title: JANUARY

b. Create a pie chart using the data in the range B10..E10. Use the same titles as in the bar chart you created in the last step. Include X-axis labels. Name and save the graph as PIE-EX1B.

c. Create a bar chart to compare each monthly expense total for each type of expense. The data you will graph is in the range F5..F8. Include X-axis labels. Also include the following titles and then name and save the graph as BAR-EX1C.
First Title: EXPENSE TYPE COMPARISON
Second Title: FOR THE MONTH OF JANUARY

d. Create a grouped bar chart comparing each expense type over the four weeks of January. Include X-axis labels and a legend. Also, include the same titles as in BAR-EX1C. When finished, name and save the graph as BAR-EX1D. The data you will graph is in the following ranges:
(1) B5..E5
(2) B6..E6
(3) B7..E7
(4) B8..E8

e. Create a stacked bar chart using the BAR-EX1D specifications. Name and save the graph as BAR-EX1E.

f. Generate a list of graph names in a range located below your spreadsheet.

g. Save the WEEKLY spreadsheet onto your Advantage Diskette and print it in both the as-displayed and cell-formulas formats.

2. Using the spreadsheet SALES stored on the Advantage Diskette, create charts that have the same characteristics as those pictured in Figure 5.22. Save each chart you create onto the Advantage Diskette.

3. Load PrintGraph and print the charts you created in exercises 1 and 2.

Figure 5.22(a)

Bar chart

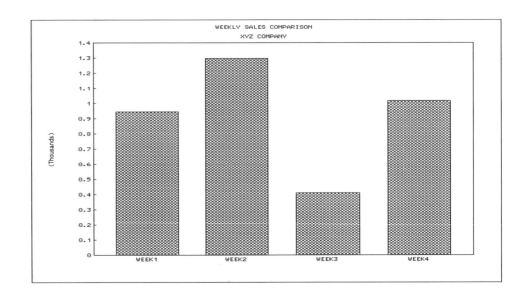

Figure 5.22(b)

Exploded pie
chart

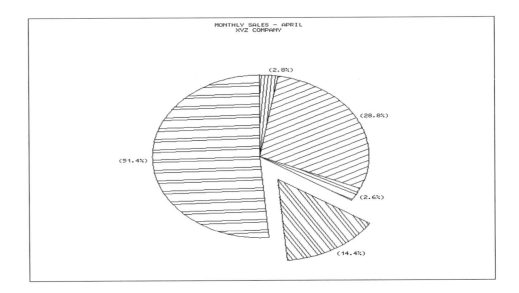

Figure 5.22(c)

Grouped bar chart:
Tennis vs. Biking
shorts

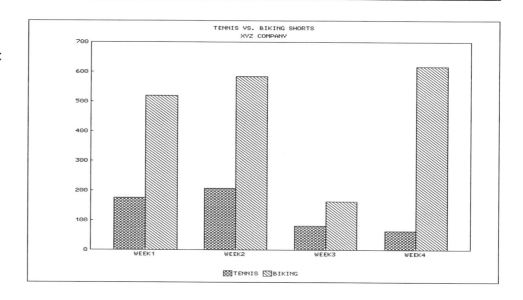

Figure 5.22(d)

Grouped bar chart:
Week1 vs. Week2

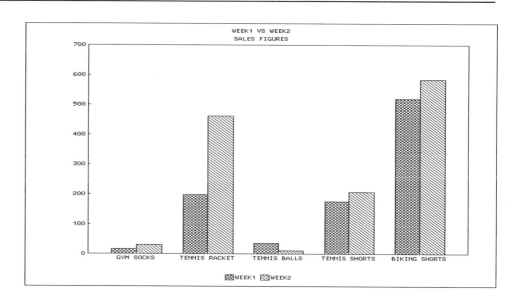

4. Retrieve XYZDEPT1 from the Advantage Diskette and then create the following charts:
   a. Create a bar chart that compares Gross Receipts and Total Expenses for January, February, and March. Include X-axis labels and a legend. Include the following titles and then name and save the chart as BAR-EX4A:
   First Title: `XYZ Company - Department 1`
   Second Title: `Receipts vs. Expenses`

b. Create a side-by-side bar chart that compares each type of expense (Accounting, Advertising, Telephone, and Travel) for January, February, and March. Include X-axis labels and a legend. Include the following titles and then name and save the chart as BAR-EX4B:
First Title: DEPARTMENT 1: WIDGETS
Second Title: 1st QUARTER EXPENSES

5. Retrieve EMPLOYED from the Advantage Diskette. Create the charts pictured in Figure 5.23. Name each chart you create and save each onto the Advantage Diskette.

Figure 5.23(a)

Grouped bar chart

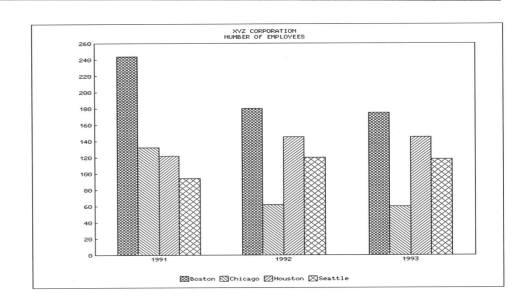

Figure 5.23(b)

Exploded pie chart

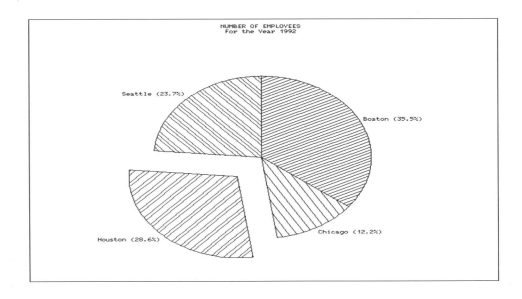

Figure 5.23(c)

Stacked bar
chart

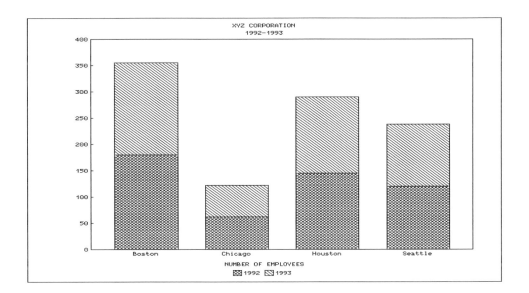

LOTUS 1-2-3 ADD-INS: ALLWAYS AND THE MACRO LIBRARY MANAGER

Not only does Lotus 1-2-3 provide a broad range of commands that enable users to create spreadsheet reports, manage databases, and present data in graphic form, but it also provides users with tools for improving spreadsheet data presentation and streamlining program use. This lesson introduces you to two important add-in software products that increase the power and flexibility of Lotus 1-2-3. (These add-ins come packaged with Lotus 1-2-3, version 2.2, but users of earlier versions of Lotus must purchase these add-in programs separately.)

PREVIEW

When you have completed this session, you will be able to:

Load add-in software programs with Lotus 1-2-3.
·
Use Allways to improve your spreadsheet's appearance.
·
Use the Macro Library Manager to simplify your use of macros.

SESSION OUTLINE

Why Is This Session Important?
Using Add-In Software
Allways Fundamentals
      How Allways Uses the Keyboard
      Enhancing a Report
      Including a Graph in a Report
Macro Library Manager Fundamentals
      Creating and Using a Macro Library
Summary
      Command Summary
Key Terms
Exercises
      Short Answer
      Hands-On

WHY IS THIS SESSION IMPORTANT?

When you purchase Lotus 2.2, you get more than the Lotus 1-2-3 spreadsheet software. Packaged with Lotus 2.2 are two add-in software programs: (1) Allways and (2) Macro Library Manager. **Add-in software** is often referred to as RAM-resident software because it is stored in RAM when the computer is on; it is also referred to as TSR (Terminate and Stay Resident) software. To "talk to," or use, this software the user issues a command to switch from Lotus 1-2-3 to one of the add-in programs.

Allways enables the user to improve the appearance of reports printed in the as-displayed format. (You learned how to print in Session 2.) The best way to understand what Allways can do is to compare a report that was printed without using any Allways commands (Figure 6.1) with one printed using a number of Allways commands (Figure 6.2). Allways made the following improvements to the spreadsheet:

1. Typeface was made larger and changed to one that is easier to read.
2. "Total" column was shaded to stand out.
3. Underlines were included in rows 2, 8, and 10.

Figure 6.1

The QUARTER1 spreadsheet. No Allways commands have been used.

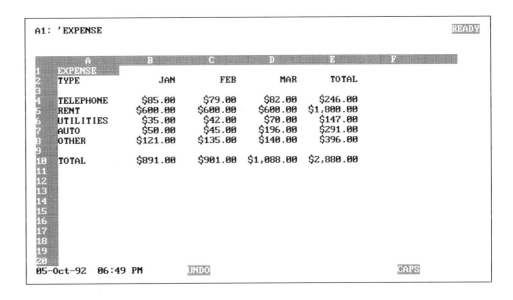

Figure 6.2

The QUARTER1
spreadsheet. Several
Allways commands
have been used.

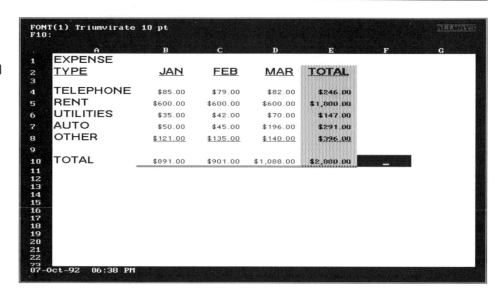

In this session we also describe the Macro Library Manager, which enables you to create a library, or table, of macros in RAM and to use any macros stored in the library in any spreadsheet that you are working with. (In Session 4 you learned how to create macros within your spreadsheets.) Many procedures, such as the save and print procedures, require almost identical keystrokes no matter what spreadsheet you are using. So instead of, for example, creating a save macro in every spreadsheet you create, you can use the save macro that is stored in the macro library. Thanks to the Macro Library Manager software you have to create macros only once, and then you can use them over and over again in your spreadsheets.

In this session you learn the fundamentals of using Allways and the Macro Library Manager. This session isn't intended to show you all there is to know about these two tools. Rather, the purpose of this session is to provide you with an overview of what these tools have to offer and to show you how to invoke these add-in software programs when working with your spreadsheets.

Before proceeding, make sure the following are true:

1. You have loaded Lotus 1-2-3 and are displaying an empty spreadsheet template on the screen.

2. Your Advantage Diskette is inserted in the drive. You will save your work onto the diskette and retrieve the files that have been created for you. (Note: The Advantage Diskette can be made by copying all the files off the instructor's Master Advantage Diskette onto a formatted diskette.)

USING ADD-IN SOFTWARE

The first step in using add-in software is to load it into RAM so that it is attached to the current application. This process is referred to as **attaching.** This must be done at the beginning of every session in which you want to use the add-in software. When you are using Lotus 1-2-3, perform the following steps to use an add-in software program:

1. The add-in must be "attached" to the current application. During this process, a list of add-in program files will appear across the top of the screen. To start Allways, you would choose the ALLWAYS.ADN file. To start the Macro Library Manager, you would choose the MACROMGR.ADN file. (Note: If one or more of these files isn't listed when you start the steps in this session, you will have to run the Allways Setup program that is stored on one of the diskettes that came with your Lotus 1-2-3 2.2 package.)

2. Once a program is attached, you have the choice of assigning a function key to the add-in. If you choose "No-Key," you will have to use the ADD-IN INVOKE command each time you want to use an add-in. If you choose 7, you can activate the add-in by holding (Alt) down and pressing (F7). If you choose 8, you can activate the add-in by holding (Alt) down and pressing (F8), and so on. These two steps must be performed at the beginning of each working session.

3. If at any point you decide you want to free up some of the RAM used by an add-in software program—for example, if you want to work with another spreadsheet that is very large—you can issue a command to "detach" the add-in, or remove it from RAM. The memory that was formerly used by the add-in will be freed for use with your spreadsheet.

ALLWAYS FUNDAMENTALS

When you use Allways to enhance a spreadsheet report, Allways creates a file that has the same name as the file you are working on but with the extension of .ALL. Your Allways specifications are saved in the .ALL file when you save the spreadsheet using the FILE SAVE command from within Lotus 1-2-3.

CAUTION: If you don't make any changes to the spreadsheet using Lotus 1-2-3 but make changes to the spreadsheet using Allways, be sure to exit Allways and then use Lotus's FILE SAVE command. The corresponding .ALL file will be updated.

CAUTION: Attach Allways before you make any substantial changes to the spreadsheet. If you don't, the .ALL file and your spreadsheet file might become mismatched, which will produce unpredictable results on your spreadsheet. For example, the wrong range of cells might appear enlarged or in boldface.

HOW ALLWAYS USES THE KEYBOARD

Allways assigns a few different commands to the function keys and also provides you with a number of accelerator keys that enable you to issue commands will fewer keystrokes.

FUNCTION KEYS
The following list shows how Allways uses the function keys:

F1 HELP This command displays the Allways help screen.

F4 REDUCE This command enables you to reduce the cells in a spreadsheet to as little as 60% of their current size.

Alt+F4 ENLARGE This command enables you to enlarge cells up to 140% of their normal size.

F5 GOTO This command enables you to move the cursor directly to any named cell or range.

F6 DISPLAY This command changes the screen from Graphics to Text mode and vice versa. In Graphics mode, what you see on the screen is almost identical to what you will see when you print the spreadsheet—that is, you will see the effect of the Allways commands. In Text mode, your spreadsheet looks like it does without using any Allways commands.

F10 GRAPH This command is used to display graphs that you have positioned in your spreadsheet. If you don't press this, the location of any graphs in your spreadsheet is indicated by cross-hatching. After you press **F10**, however, you can see the actual graph. In this session, we lead you through how to include a graph in a report.

ACCELERATOR KEYS
All accelerator keys correspond to a sequence of Allways keystrokes. These keys provide you with command shortcuts so you don't have to press as many keys to give common commands. Each accelerator key is activated by first holding down **Alt**. For example, instead of having to use approximately four keys to make something appear bold, you only have to hold **Alt** down and type B. Following is a list of the Allways accelerator keys:

Alt+B	Boldface (Set, Clear)
Alt+G	Grid Lines (On, Off)
Alt+L	Lines (Outline, All, None)
Alt+S	Shading (Light, Dark, Solid, None)
Alt+U	Underline (Single, Double, None)

(Alt)+1   Set font 1
(Alt)+2   Set font 2
.
.   etc.
.
(Alt)+8   Set font 8

(A font is a particular style of typeface in a particular size.)

ENHANCING A REPORT

In this section you will enhance the spreadsheet named QUARTER1 (Figure 6.1) which is similar to a spreadsheet that you created in Session 2. This spreadsheet is stored on your Advantage Diskette. To initiate Allways and make the enhancements, perform the following steps:

1. Before attaching Allways to Lotus 1-2-3, you will disable the Undo feature (described in Session 1) to free up more RAM for the Allways add-in. Perform the following steps to disable the UNDO command:
    To initiate Menu mode:
    TYPE: /
    CHOOSE: Worksheet, Global, Default
    CHOOSE: Other, Undo, Disable
    To exit from this menu:
    CHOOSE: Quit

Quick Reference

Disabling the Undo Feature

By disabling the UNDO command, you make more RAM available for use with a Lotus add-in.
1. Initiate Menu mode.
2. CHOOSE: Worksheet, Global, Default
3. CHOOSE: Other, Undo, Disable
4. To exit from this menu:
    CHOOSE: Quit

---

2. Retrieve the file named QUARTER1 from the Advantage Diskette. (The procedure for retrieving was described in Session 2.)

3. In this step Allways is attached to Lotus 1-2-3, assigned [F7], and invoked:
    TYPE: /
    To choose the Add-In option:
    CHOOSE: Add-in, Attach
    PRESS: *cursor-movement keys to highlight the ALLWAYS.ADN file*
    PRESS: [Enter]
    To assign [F7] to Allways:
    CHOOSE: 7
    To choose the Invoke option:
    CHOOSE: Invoke
    PRESS: *cursor-movement keys to highlight ALLWAYS*
    PRESS: [Enter]

    The screen should look like Figure 6.3. At this point, Allways assumes you will use the font Triumvirate 10 point (see top upper-left of screen), which is the font Allways will use unless you change the assumption. ("Points" designate the size of a font, or set of characters in a given typeface. For example, 12-point characters are larger than 10-point characters.)

Figure 6.3

A view of the
QUARTER1
spreadsheet
after Allways
has been
attached

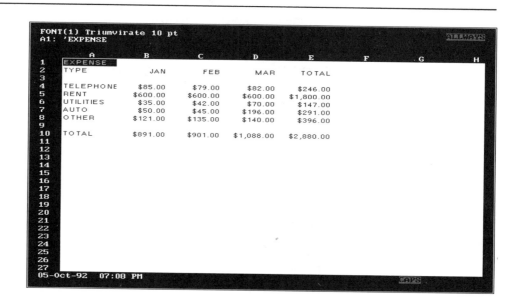

Quick Reference

*Attaching an Add-In
and Assigning a
Function Key*

1. Initiate Menu mode.
2. CHOOSE: Add-in, Attach
3. Highlight the name of the add-in you want to attach, and then press [Enter].
4. To assign a function key to the add-in, type 7, 8, 9, or 10. The add-in will be assigned to the corresponding function key ([F7], [F8] [F9], or [F10]).
5. CHOOSE: Invoke
6. Highlight the name of the add-in you want to invoke, and then press [Enter].

4. In this step you will change the headings in the range A1..E2 so they are larger.

PRESS: *cursor-movement keys to position the cursor in cell A1*

To highlight the range you want to work on:

TYPE: .

Note the ANC (anchor) indicator in the bottom-center of the screen.

PRESS: *cursor-movement keys to highlight the range A1..E2*

To make the headings appear larger, you're going to choose the Triumvirate 14 point. Perform the following steps:

TYPE: /

CHOOSE: Format, Font

The screen should look like Figure 6.4.

Figure 6.4

Allways lets you choose from a number of different typefaces and sizes. The larger the point size you use to format a range of cells, the larger the cell contents will appear.

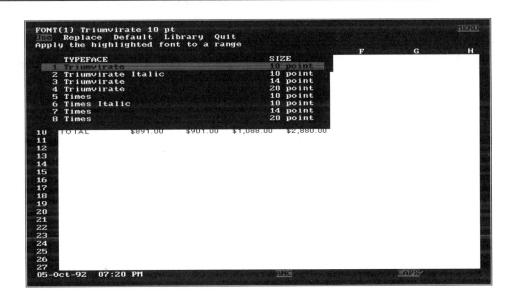

To choose the option Triumvirate 14 point:

PRESS: ⬇ *twice*

PRESS: Enter

The screen should look like Figure 6.5.

Figure 6.5

The headings in
the range A1..E2
were enlarged by
choosing the
Triumvirate 14
point option.

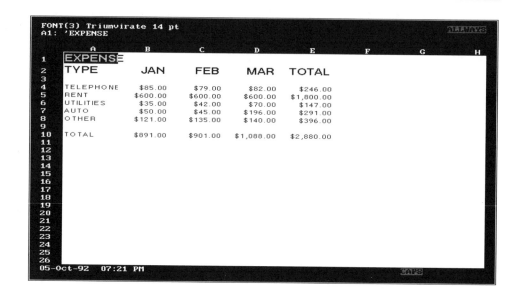

Quick Reference

*Choosing a Different
Font (Type Size)*

1. Position the cursor at the beginning of the range that you want to alter.
2. To anchor the beginning of the range:
   TYPE: .
3. Highlight the range you want to alter.
4. Initiate Menu mode.
5. CHOOSE: Format, Font
6. Highlight the font you want to use and press (Enter).

5. In this step you will change the headings in the range A4..A10 so they are larger.
   To highlight A4..A10:
   PRESS: *cursor-movement keys to put the cursor in cell A4*
   PRESS: .
   PRESS: (↓) *six times*
   To initiate Menu mode:
   TYPE: /
   CHOOSE: Format, Font
   To choose the option Triumvirate 14 point:
   PRESS: (↓) *twice*
   PRESS: (Enter)
   The screen should look like Figure 6.6. Note that column A isn't wide enough to display the larger text.

Figure 6.6

The headings in the range A4..A10 were enlarged by choosing the Triumvirate 14 point option. Note that column A must be widened to accommodate the larger text.

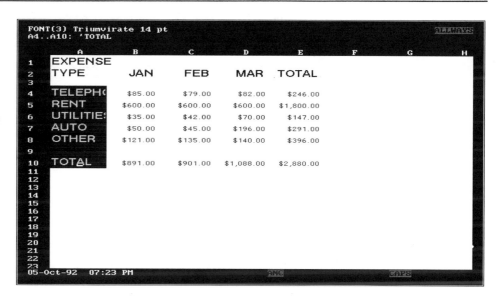

Quick Reference

Unanchoring a Range

Allways often remembers the previous range you defined in case you want to perform more than one command on the range. If this isn't what you want:

PRESS: [Esc]

---

6. To widen column A:
    TYPE: /
    CHOOSE: <u>W</u>orksheet, <u>C</u>olumn, <u>S</u>et
    PRESS: [→] *six times*
    PRESS: [Enter]
    The screen should look like Figure 6.7.

Quick Reference

Widening a Column

1. Position the cursor in the column to be widened.
2. Initiate Menu mode.
3. CHOOSE: <u>W</u>orksheet, <u>C</u>olumn, <u>S</u>et
4. Use the cursor-movement keys to widen the column to the desired width, or type in a number (corresponding to the desired width) directly.
5. Press: [Enter]

Figure 6.7

Column A was
widened.

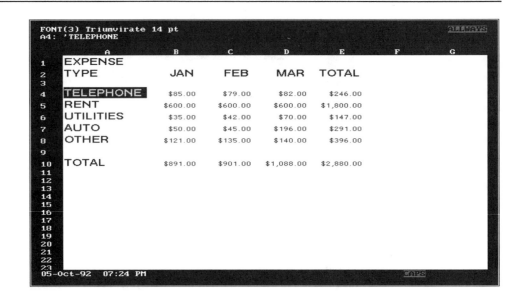

7. In this step you will underline the headings in row 2. In addition, you will
    double-underline the totals in row 10.
    PRESS: *cursor-movement keys to position the cursor in cell A2*
    TYPE: .
    PRESS: ⏵ *four times*
    To initiate Menu mode:
    PRESS: /
    CHOOSE: Format, Underline, Single
    PRESS: ⏷ *once*
    The range A2..E2 should now be displaying with underlines.

Quick Reference

Adding Underlines

1. Position the cursor where you want the underlining to begin.
2. To anchor the beginning of the range:
    TYPE: .
3. Highlight the range to be altered.
4. Initiate Menu mode.
5. CHOOSE: Format, Underline
6. Choose the Single or Double option.

8. To enter an underline in row 8:
    PRESS: *cursor-movement keys to position the cursor in cell B8*
    To highlight the range B8..E8:
    TYPE: .
    PRESS: ⏵ *three times*
    To initiate Menu mode:
    PRESS: /

CHOOSE: Format, Underline, Single

9. To enter a double-underline beneath the totals in row 10:
   PRESS: *cursor-movement keys to position the cursor in cell B10*
   To highlight the range:
   TYPE: .
   PRESS: → *three times*
   To initiate Menu mode:
   PRESS: /
   CHOOSE: Format, Underline, Double
   PRESS: → *once*
   The screen should look like Figure 6.8.

Figure 6.8

Underlines have
been included in
the spreadsheet.

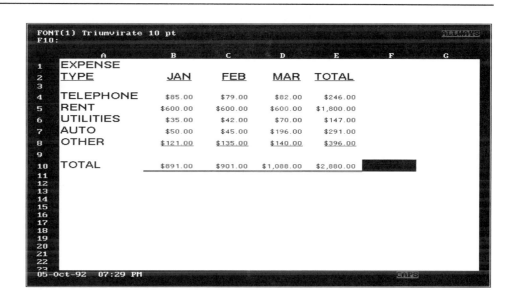

10. To draw attention to the totals in column E (E2..E10), you will shade them in
    this step. To unanchor the previous range:
    PRESS: *cursor-movement keys to position the cursor in cell E2*
    To highlight the range E2..E10:
    TYPE: .
    PRESS: ↓ *eight times to highlight E2..E10*
    To initiate Menu mode:
    TYPE: /
    CHOOSE: Format, Shade, Dark
    PRESS: → *once*
    The screen should look like Figure 6.2.

Quick Reference

Adding Shading

1. Position the cursor in the beginning of the range that should be shaded.
2. To anchor the beginning of the range:
   TYPE: .
3. Initiate Menu mode.
4. CHOOSE: Format, Shade, Dark

---

11. In this step you will print the QUARTER1 spreadsheet.
    To position the cursor in cell A1:
    PRESS: [Home]
    To bring up the Allways menu:
    TYPE: /
    CHOOSE: Print, Range, Set
    PRESS: *cursor-movement keys to highlight the range A1..E10*
    PRESS: [Enter]
    CHOOSE: Go

Quick Reference

Printing the Allways Report

1. Position the cursor in the beginning of the print range.
2. To bring up the Allways menu:
   TYPE: /
3. CHOOSE: Print, Range, Set
4. Highlight the range you want to print, and then press [Enter].
5. CHOOSE: Go

---

12. In this step you will return to Lotus 1-2-3 to save the spreadsheet onto the Advantage Diskette. When you save the spreadsheet, the corresponding .ALL file that was created as a result of your recent Allways activities will be saved with the spreadsheet. To exit Allways and return to Lotus 1-2-3:
    PRESS: [Alt]+[F7]

13. The Lotus 1-2-3 spreadsheet should be displaying on the screen.
    TYPE: /
    CHOOSE: File, Save
    To save the spreadsheet using the same name:
    PRESS: [Enter]
    CHOOSE: Replace

Quick Reference

*Exiting to Lotus
and Saving*

1. To exit Allways and return to Lotus 1-2-3, either press [Alt] with a designated function key, or press [Esc] until you see the Lotus 1-2-3 spreadsheet.
2. Initiate Menu mode.
3. CHOOSE: File, Save
4. To save the spreadsheet using the same name:
    PRESS: [Enter]
5. CHOOSE: Replace

INCLUDING A GRAPH IN A REPORT

To include a graph in a report, the graph you want to include must be stored in a .PIC file on your disk. You created a number of .PIC files in Session 5 when you used the GRAPH SAVE command to save your graph specifications. In this section you will copy the PIECHART.PIC file (you created a file like this in Session 5) into the range A15..F35 (in the QUARTER1 spreadsheet).

1. To activate Allways:
    PRESS: [Alt]+[F7]

2. To copy the PIECHART.PIC graph into the current spreadsheet:
    PRESS: *cursor-movement keys to position the cursor in cell A15*
    To initiate Menu mode:
    TYPE: /
    CHOOSE: Graph, Add
    PRESS: *cursor-movement keys to highlight PIECHART.PIC*
    PRESS: [Enter]
    PRESS: *cursor-movement keys to highlight the range A15..F35*
    PRESS: [Enter]
    The screen should look like Figure 6.9. *Note: If you are viewing hatching on the screen, press* [F10] *to display the graph.*
    CHOOSE: Quit

3. To print the spreadsheet with the included graph:
    PRESS: /
    CHOOSE: Print, Range, Set
    To include the pie chart in the print range:
    PRESS: *cursor-movement keys to highlight the range A1..E35*
    PRESS: [Enter]
    CHOOSE: Go

Figure 6.9

A pie chart has
been added to
the QUARTER1
spreadsheet.

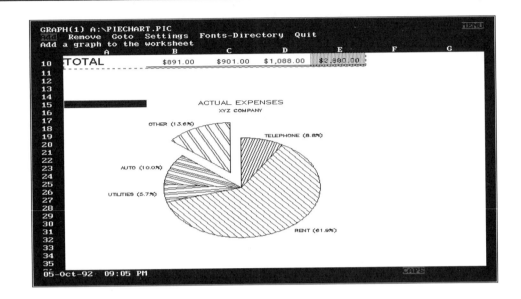

Quick Reference

*Including a Graph
in a Report*

1. Attach the Allways add-in.
2. Position the cursor where you want the graph to be positioned in the spreadsheet.
3. Initiate Menu mode.
4. CHOOSE: Graph, Add
5. Highlight the name of the graphics file you want to include in the spreadsheet, and then press (Enter).
6. Highlight the range of cells where the graph should be positioned and then press (Enter).
7. CHOOSE: Quit
8. If necessary, press the Graph key ((F10)) to see the graph and not the hatching.

---

4. To return to Lotus 1-2-3 and to then save the report:
    PRESS: (Alt)+(F7)
    The Lotus 1-2-3 spreadsheet should be displaying on the screen.
    TYPE: /
    CHOOSE: File, Save
    To save the spreadsheet using the same name:
    PRESS: (Enter)
    CHOOSE: Replace

MACRO LIBRARY MANAGER FUNDAMENTALS

The Macro Library Manager enables you to create libraries of macros, store them to disk, and use up to 10 of them with any spreadsheet you are working on. This capability can save you time because you don't have to create the same macros over and over in different spreadsheets. A **macro library** is a range that has been moved by the Macro Library Manager from a worksheet and then stored in a file with the extension of .MLB (called a **library file**); at the same time the macro library is stored in RAM. This range can contain one or more macros, data, or both macros and data. To use the Macro Library Manager you must first attach it to Lotus 1-2-3 just as you attached Allways to Lotus 1-2-3. The steps involved with creating and using a macro library include:

1. Attach the Macro Library Manager to Lotus 1-2-3.

2. The spreadsheet that contains the data or procedures that you want to include in the macro library must be retrieved into RAM.

3. Use the Macro Library Manager SAVE command to give a name to the library and specify what range of cells you want the library file to contain. When the SAVE command is issued, the Macro Library Manager removes the range of cells you specify from your spreadsheet. The range is stored in the library file on your disk and in RAM.

4. To use a macro that is stored in a macro library, simply execute the macro as you would normally—for example, by holding (Alt) down and tapping the letter S to save a spreadsheet. In other words, execute the macros the same way you would if they were still stored in the spreadsheet. Lotus knows to look in the macro library because the Macro Library Manager is attached.

5. If you exit the current spreadsheet and retrieve another spreadsheet, the macro library remains in RAM. Therefore, you can use its contents on the newly retrieved spreadsheet.

When the Macro Library Manager is first invoked, the following menu options appear:

*   *Load*. Loads a copy of the contents of a macro library file (that is stored on the disk) into RAM.

*   *Save*. Saves a specified range of cells into a library file with the extension of .MLB and copies the range of cells into another area of RAM. Deletes the range of cells from the spreadsheet.

- *Edit*. Copies a macro library into an empty range in your spreadsheet so you can make changes to it. Before using this command, make sure the cursor is in an empty area of the spreadsheet; otherwise the contents of the macro library will overwrite cells that contain data. After making changes, save the edited range using the Macro Library Manager SAVE command. You will be asked if you want to overwrite the old macro library with the updated macro library.

- *Remove*. Removes a macro library from RAM.

- *Name-List*. Copies a list of the range names contained in a macro library into the spreadsheet. Make sure the cursor is in an empty portion of the spreadsheet before using this command; otherwise the list of names will overwrite cells that contain data.

CREATING AND USING A MACRO LIBRARY

In this section you will retrieve a copy of the BILLS-EX spreadsheet that is stored on the Advantage Diskette. A save macro and two print macros are stored in the range AA3..AA9 (Figure 6.10). You will store these macros in a macro library.

Perform the following steps:

1. Retrieve a copy of BILLS-EX from the Advantage Diskette. (The procedure for retrieving a file was described in Session 2.)

2. To attach the Macro Library Manager and assign it to (F8) (so that you can invoke the Macro Library Manager by holding down (Alt) and pressing (F8)):
   TYPE: /
   CHOOSE: Add-in, Attach
   PRESS: *cursor-movement keys to highlight the MACROMGR.ADN*
   PRESS: (Enter)
   To assign the Macro Library Manager to (F8):
   CHOOSE: 8
   To quit to Ready mode:
   CHOOSE: Quit

3. Before creating a macro library that contains the range AA3..AA9, first position the cursor on the beginning of the range you want to move into the macro library—namely, cell AA3.

Figure 6.10

The save macro and the two print macros will be moved into the macro library.

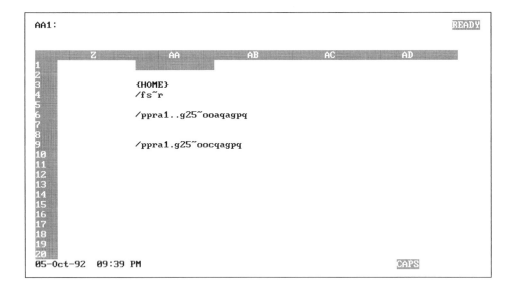

4. In the following steps you will create a macro library named MACROLIB. To invoke the Macro Library Manager:
   PRESS: Alt + F8
   CHOOSE: Save
   To specify the name of the library file:
   TYPE: MACROLIB
   PRESS: Enter
   To highlight the range AA3..AA9:
   PRESS: *cursor-movement keys to highlight the range AA3..AA9*
   PRESS: Enter
   When prompted if you want to specify a password:
   CHOOSE: No
   Note that the cells in the range AA3..AA9 are now empty. The contents of these cells are stored in a library file on the disk named MACROLIB.MLB and also in RAM.

5. At this point you can execute the macros that are stored in the macro library using normal procedures—that is, by holding Alt down and tapping the letter S, P, or C (you created macros like these in Session 4). In fact, if you exit the current spreadsheet and retrieve another spreadsheet you can still use these same macros.

6. So that your macros remain in this spreadsheet, don't save the BILLS-EX spreadsheet. To exit Lotus 1-2-3:
   TYPE: /
   CHOOSE: Quit, Yes, Yes

Quick Reference	1.	Attach and invoke the Macro Library Manager.
	2.	CHOOSE: <u>S</u>ave
Creating a Macro	3.	TYPE: *a name for your library file*
Library		PRESS: (Enter)
	4.	Highlight the cells in your spreadsheet that contain the macros to be included in the macro library, and then press (Enter).
	5.	Specify whether you want to create a password for the library.
	6.	The cells in your spreadsheet that contained the macro should now be empty.

SUMMARY

In this session, you learned about two add-in programs that can be used with Lotus 1-2-3, version 2.2, namely Allways and the Macro Library Manager. An add-in program can be used after it is attached to Lotus 1-2-3 using the ADD-IN ATTACH command.

Allways provides commands that enable you to include desktop publishing characteristics in your spreadsheets. For example, you can include such features as shading, boldfacing, and underlining to emphasize certain cells in your spreadsheet. In addition, you can use variable fonts and type sizes.

The Macro Library Manager enables you to store frequently used macros in a separate file and then use them repeatedly in different spreadsheets. The Macro Library Manager frees you from creating macros that are very similar in multiple spreadsheets.

COMMAND SUMMARY

The table on the next page provides a list of the commands and procedures covered in this session.

Table 6.1	Disable the UNDO feature	/, Worksheet, Global, Default, Other, Undo, Disable, Quit
Command Summary	Attach an add-in and assign a function key	/, Add-in, Attach, highlight the name of the file to attach, (Enter), type a number corresponding to a function key
	Invoke an add-in	If a function key has been assigned: Hold (Alt) down and press the function key that corresponds to the number you typed when attaching the add-in
		If "No-key" has been assigned: /, Add-in, Invoke, highlight the add-in to invoke, (Enter)
	Choose a different font (Allways)	Position the cursor at the beginning of the range to be altered, type . to anchor the beginning of the range, highlight the range to be altered, /, Format, Font, highlight the appropriate font, (Enter)
	Unanchor a range (Allways)	(Esc)
	Widen a column (Allways)	Position the cursor in the column to be widened, /, Worksheet, Column, Set-width, press (→) to mark the new width, (Enter)
	Add underlines (Allways)	Position the cursor where underlining should begin, type . to anchor the beginning of the range, highlight the range to be underlined, /, Format, Underline, choose Single or Double
	Add shading (Allways)	Position the cursor where shading should begin, type . to anchor the beginning of the range, highlight the range to be shaded, /, Format, Shade, choose Light, Dark or Solid
	Print an Allways report	Position the cursor at the beginning of the print range, /, Print, Range, Set, highlight the range you want to print, (Enter), Go
	Exit Allways to Lotus	Press (Esc) until you see the spreadsheet or hold (Alt) down and type the function key you picked when attaching Allways

(continued)

Table 6.1	Include a graph in a report (Allways)	Position the cursor where the graph should be positioned, /, Graph, Add, highlight the name of the graph to be included, (Enter), highlight the range of cells that will contain the graph, (Enter), Quit, if necessary press (F10) to see the graph
Command Summary (concluded)	Create a macro library	Attach and then invoke the Macro Library Manager add-in, Save, type a name for the library file, (Enter), highlight the cells in your spreadsheet that contain the macros to be included in the macro library, (Enter), specify whether you want to include a password for the library, the cells in your spreadsheet that contained the macro should now be empty.

KEY TERMS

add-in software   Ram-resident software that is used in conjunction with applications software to provide additional capabilities.

attaching   The first step in using add-in software with Lotus 1-2-3: loading it into RAM so that it can be used with the current application; this must be done at the beginning of every session in which you want to use the add-in software.

library file   File that contains one or more macros created using the Macro Library add-in utility.

macro library   In Lotus 1-2-3, a collection of macros in RAM that can be used by more than one spreadsheet.

EXERCISES

SHORT ANSWER

1. What does it mean to "attach" an add-in program?
2. What is Allways used for?
3. What is the Macro Library Manager used for?
4. What is the difference between attaching and invoking an add-in program?
5. Why is it often necessary to disable the UNDO feature before using an add-in program?
6. Using Allways, what is the procedure for underlining a range of cells?

7. Using Allways, what is the procedure for boldfacing a range of cells?
8. Why is it important to save your 1-2-3 spreadsheet after using Allways to enhance a report?
9. After attaching an add-in, you are prompted to either assign a function key to the application or not to. What does this mean?
10. How can the Macro Library Manager save you time?

HANDS-ON

1. Retrieve INCOME from the Advantage Diskette. Use Allways to perform the following steps:
   a. Boldface all column labels, row labels, and all underlines.
   b. Change the font of cell A1 to Triumvirate 14 point.
   c. Change the font of all other text and labels to Times 10 point.
   d. Shade the data in rows 8 and 18 using the Light option.
   e. Shade the data in row 20 using the Dark option.
   f. Print the Allways report.
   g. Display your spreadsheet and save INCOME onto the Advantage Diskette.

2. Retrieve SALES from the Advantage Diskette. Perform the following steps:
   a. Use Allways to enhance the report to look like Figure 6.11. (Hint: Use Times 10 point to format the spreadsheet data and labels.)

Figure 6.11

The SALES spreadsheet has been enhanced using Allways.

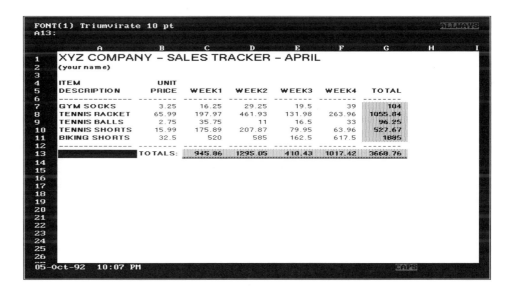

   b. Print the Allways report.
   c. Save SALES onto your Advantage Diskette.

3. Retrieve YEAR from the Advantage Diskette.
   a. Use Allways to make this report as effective as possible.
   b. Print the Allways report.
   c. Save YEAR onto your Advantage Diskette.

4. Retrieve XYZDEPT1 from the Advantage Diskette and then perform the following steps:
   a. Boldface all column labels and row labels.
   b. Change the font of cell A1 to Triumvirate 14 point.
   c. Change the font of all other text and labels to Times 10 point.
   d. Shade the data in rows 5 and 13 using the Light option.
   e. Shade the data in row 15 using the Dark option.
   f. Print the Allways report.
   g. Display your spreadsheet and save INCOME onto the Advantage Diskette.